SHOOTING
FROM THE
HIP

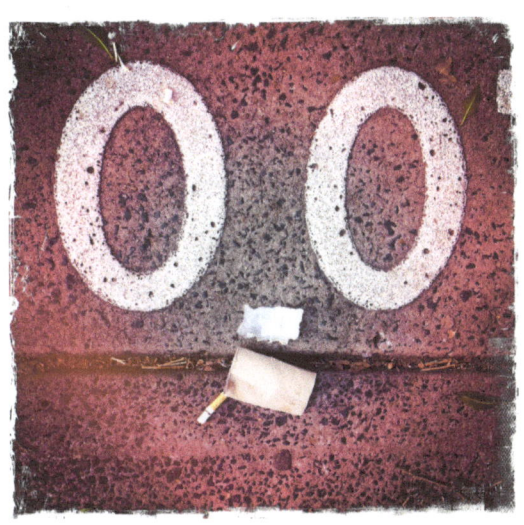

Three Years of IPhone Street Photography
as Captured and Commented on by

Orlando Luminere

Legals

Shooting from the Hip

3 Years of iPhone Photography as Captured and Commented on by

Orlando Luminere

ISBN:13 978-0-9944189-0-6

10 9 8 7 6 5 4 3 2 1
International English Print Version
Copyright 2016 Orlando Luminere

This book is printed by Create Space, an amazon.com Company.

Warning, disclaimer and limitation of liability Information in this book is provided on an "as is" basis and the reader is expected to make their own informed decisions based on due diligence, research and common sense. Neither the author or publisher shall be liable or responsible in any way to any person or entity arising from the use, misuse or any ideas or actions or loss or damages arising from this book.

Open source fonts are used in this book .

Special Sales and Authors Events

The author may be contacted via his website:
www.luminere.com

Acknowledgements

Shot entirely with the *Hipstamatic* app on *iPhone* (various iterations of both), this book was born from these technologies and the many people who created them. Thanks to you all for creating these photographic tools that let me see the world in such a new and refreshing way.

In preparing this book, I must give particular thanks to my daughter for discarding her old iPhone in my direction. Also to my artistic colleague Vivianne for suggesting I assemble these images into a book.

This book has been edited by language and punctuation geek, Angela J Williams.

Additional editing, hugs and art advice provided by Denise Hume.

Of course, I am indebted to all the photographers, designers and artists who have come before me, for they have made art and photography the rich expressive field it is today.

Finally, I am always in wonderment and appreciation of the world, for stopping long enough for me to get a photograph, or if need be, moving quickly enough for me to get a photograph.

Orlando Luminere
2016

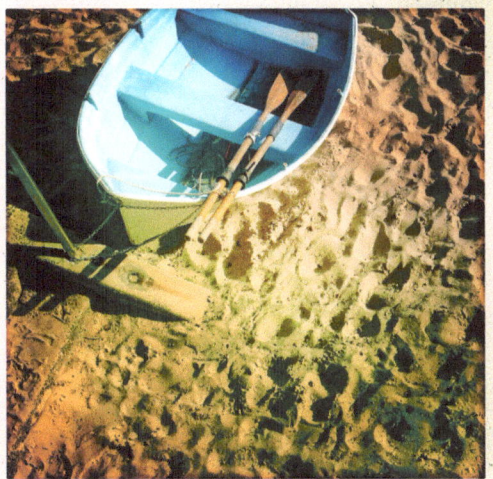

Contents

Look at the pictures. Read the text. Like it and share it. There is a joy to photography, share the joy!

As you will soon discover, this book tends towards opinionation and occasional digression. It is factual, mostly, except for the photographs, which can never factually represent our reality.

At times I drop names and use terms you might have learned if you attended art school and did anything other than party and play with charcoal. Where I do this I put the name or term in *Italics*. Most of these find their way into the index.

The *Italics* give you the opportunity to look up the term in a book, or more probably, on the internet where you will have to sift through all the informative, mis-informative, correct and incorrect content it provides.

Primarily, this book is meant to be fun and inspire all photographers to get out there, create and enjoy. Whether you use a mobile phone or the best professional equipment, which costs more than a farm in Bulgaria, I hope this book has something for you.

This book is a three year travelogue of the mobile part of my photographic life. It is a journey in which I share its stories and explain how images work or don't, and for example, why one day I was the only person to see a photograph that *Henri Cartier-Bresson* also saw and photographed back in 1932.

I do not get into techniques. The *Hipstamatic* app has a yellow button, press it and the app does the rest, much as *Kodak* did the rest for photographers back in 1889. I do not get into details of filters and effects used, as this book is mostly about finding photographs in the first place.

My intention is to push you towards engaging your brain before pressing the button. To help you do this, I will cajole you and sometimes try to bribe you with over-sweetened *eye candy*

Will the Real Photographer Step Forward

Wandering around the city one dull day, *iPhone* with *Hipstamatic* app and my "proper" camera nowhere to be seen, I was confronted by a wall of type insinuating that by using a mobile phone as a camera, I was not a real photographer but a fake.

Being both insulted and intrigued by this proposition, I recorded it on my *iPhone* (see opposite).

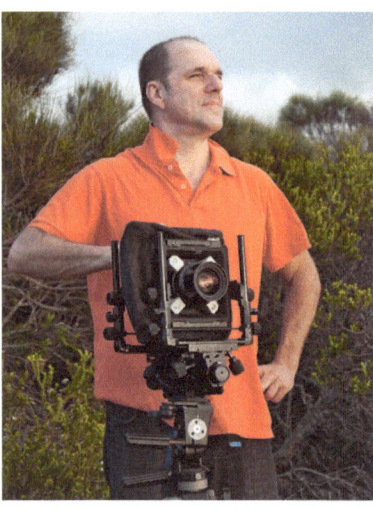

Is mobile photography a fake? I don't care. I inhabit a derivative of the *F64 School of Photography* with a digital adaption of the *large format*

cameras of the 1930's that were very large, very slow and exacting to use, and recorded incredible detail.

There's me with my big camera, paying homage to *Ansell Adams* and *Edward Weston*. Paradoxically, I also inhabit the ubiquitously modern space of mobile phone photography with social media as its gallery.

It wasn't always like this, but several years ago my daughter gave me her old *iPhone* and my photographic life was irrevocably changed. In the first month I had clocked up over 2,500 photographs.

What a difference. I used to create 200 *megapixel* photographs that *pixel peepers* could not fault (or sod them for being irrelevant if they did).

I delighted in cameras that had ten different ways the lens might be placed in relation to the image sensor. I was the complete opposite of *point and shoot,* smart photographer and dumb camera?

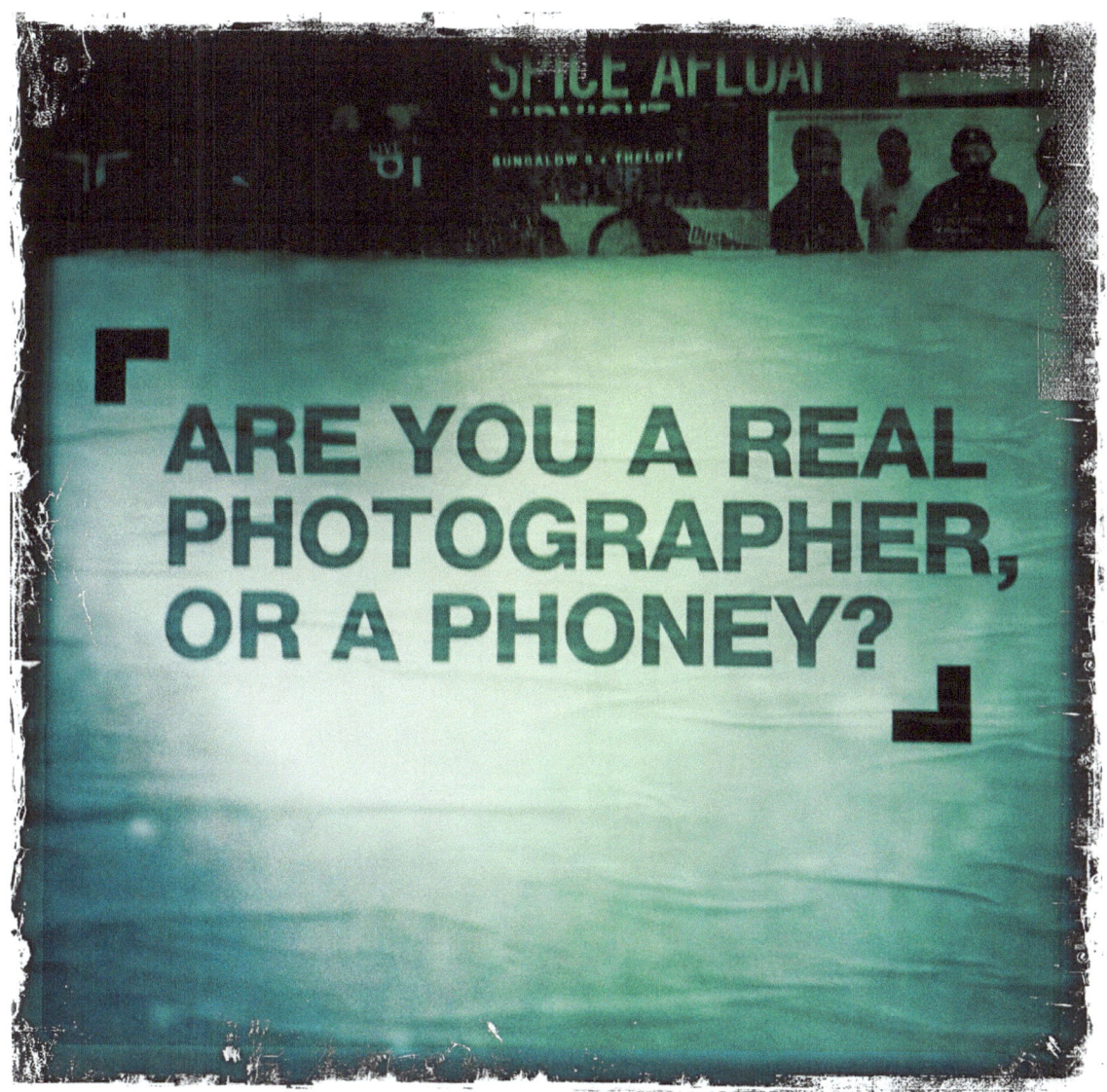

Poster by Olympus, makers of proper cameras, just ask them.

Enter the *iPhone* and the *Hipstamatic* app. The first versions of the app offered NO CONTROL whatsoever! All you could do was select a filter and press the yellow button. You even had to *zoom with your feet*!

The images were terrible. The colour was tragic, detail was gargantuan in its absence, and the splotches and grain were totally abhorrent.

Yet, somehow because of all this, the photographs were utterly fantastic and refreshing! I was hooked.

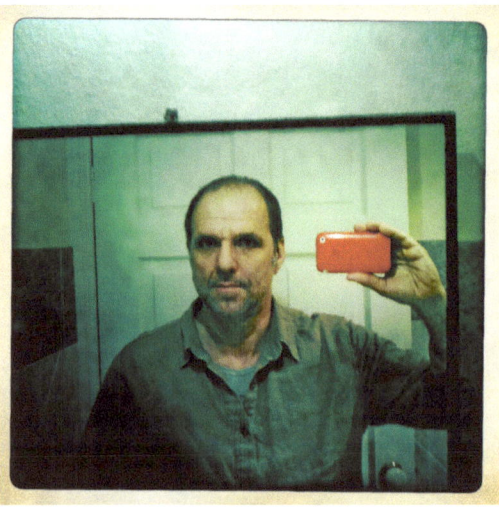

Not paying homage to anyone.

Now the Hipstamatic app allows camera adjustments and extensive post-photography editing.

What this photographic tool does is help dissociate the photographer from the notion that they are recording reality.

This is one of the major fallacies. Photographs never record reality, meaning, the reality we perceive.

At best cameras trick us into thinking they do. By breaking the nexus between photography and *representationalism*, these indistinct *iPhone* photographs become designs and plays of colour, shape, line, texture and tone.

These elements and a few more, are the building blocks of visual art that are (or should be) taught in all painting, drawing, design and photography schools.

For example, opposite, we have line, shape, tone, texture and plenty of dialectic between the *positive and negative spaces* of the image.

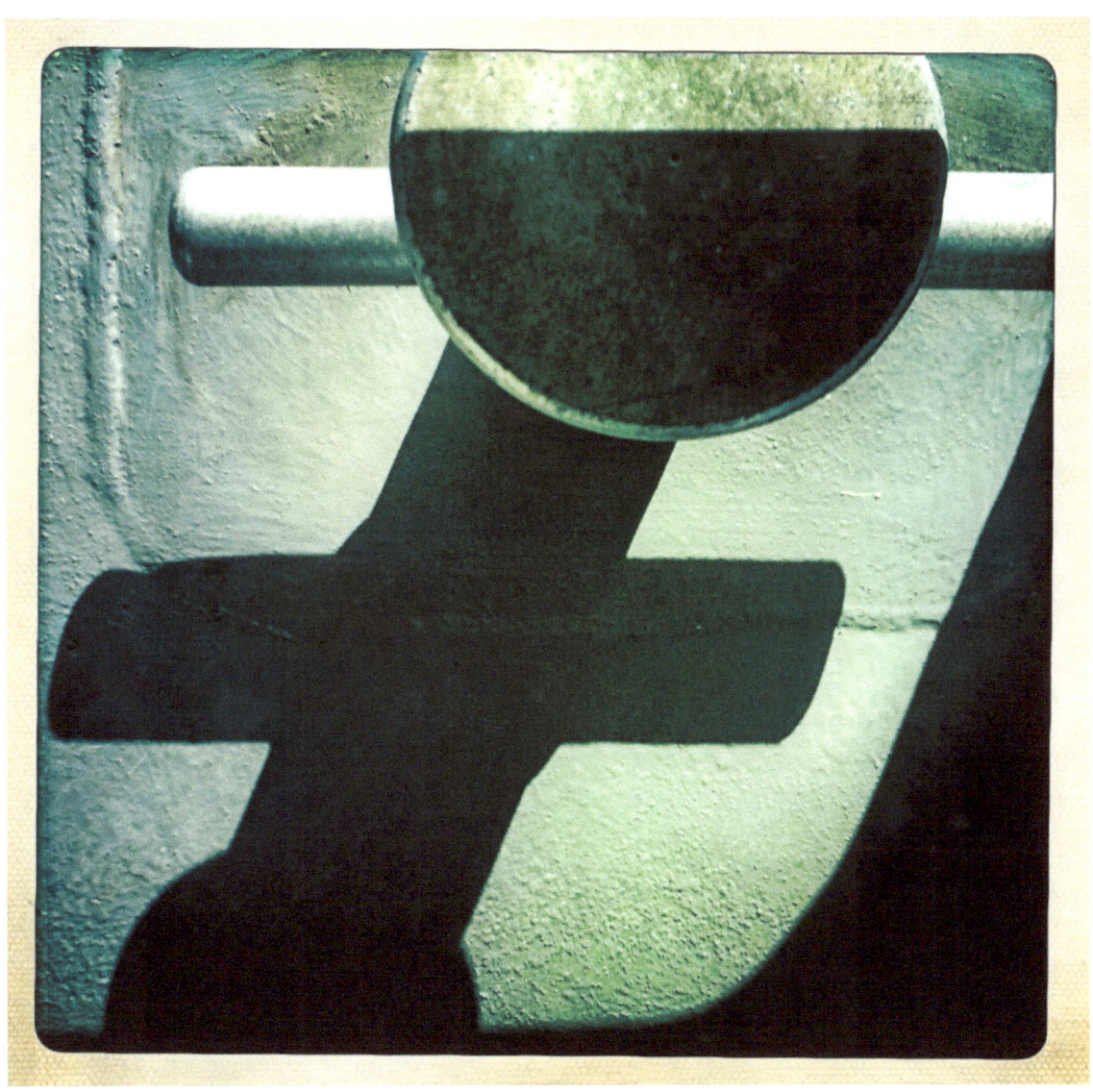

Noughts and Crosses, also known as *Tic-Tac-Toe*, can also be a photographic game.

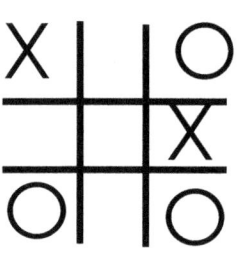

X's turn now. X is about to lose unless O gets distracted

When I started using my *iPhone* with the *Hipstamatic* app, I couldn't see how the images had any substance, integrity or credibility of their own.

They lacked resolution, detail, often had excessive noise, and were not colour accurate. I was forced to give up on *representationalism*. Then I noticed how the camera rendered shapes and I liked it. So I started photographing shapes.

After a life of learning every corner of photography, including once, reading *Ansel Adams'* trilogy, *"The Camera, The Negative, The Print"* cover to cover as self-imposed penance for wrongly exposing a piece of *5x4 inch Black and White (B&W) film*, I had become an *iPhone* photographer who went out and photographed shapes.

From a purist perspective I had become a tragic. I was told I was a *sick puppy* (not for the first time in my life, incidentally). But, I was enjoying myself!

As I couldn't see how any of these photographs could stand on their own, I played *Noughts and Crosses* with them. I used an elastic set of rules in which I also had to make the colour work.

Those who know about composition will see I had created a rigid *Rule of Thirds* grid. Usually the *Rule of Thirds* applies to elements of a single image, but in this case, I used separate images to construct this framework.

In the assemblage right, you might see that circles have won with both diagonals which form one big X. This reveals my preference for circles over X's as shapes to photograph.

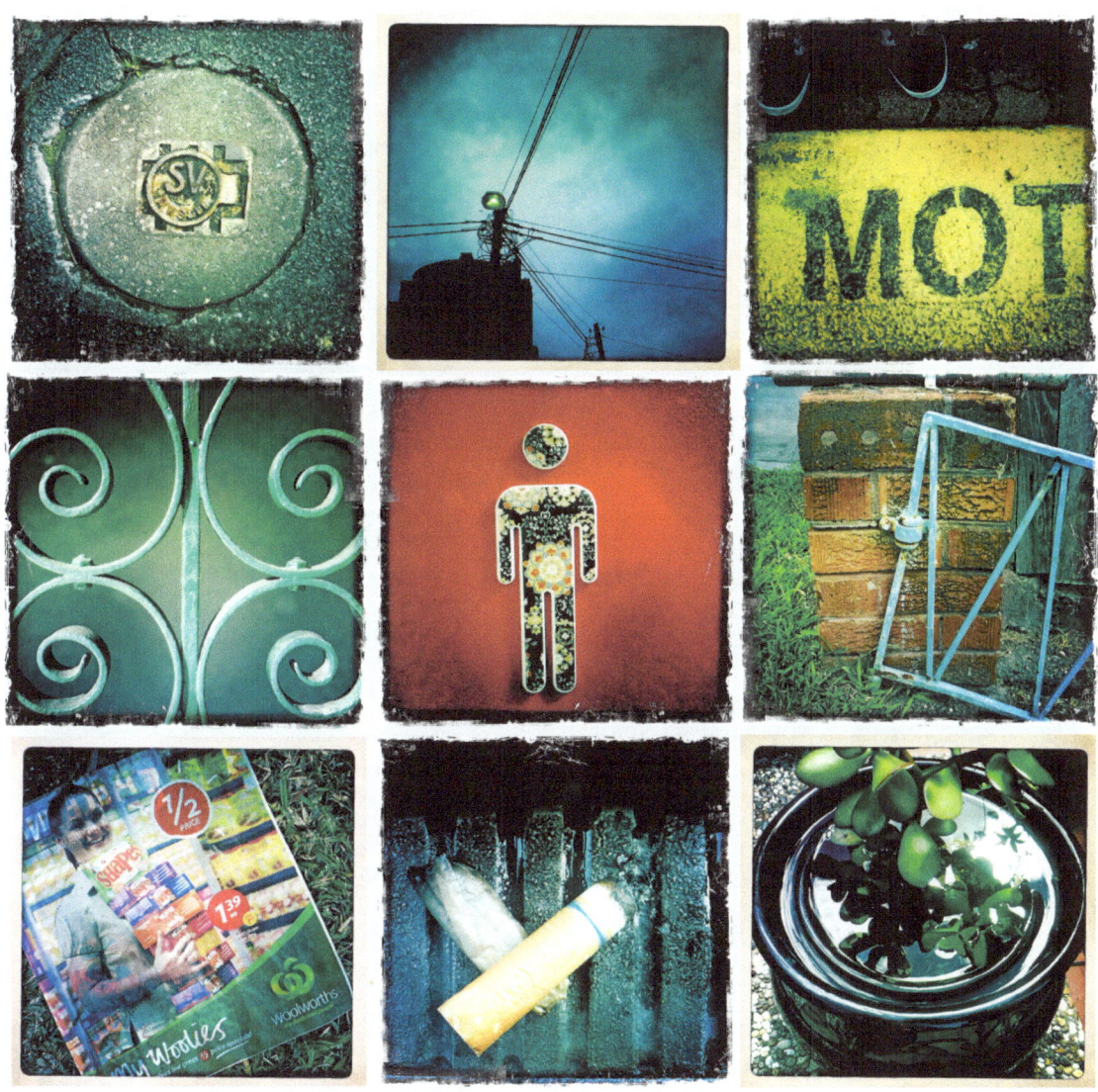

Next it rained and rained and rained, so I created a *pictorial narrative* with rain as its underlying *motif*.

In the image collection right, there is a sequence of droplets, urinal and cigarette butts. About half of the world's population see this more often than they see a blue moon.

The urinal is a reference to *Marcel Duchamp* who submitted one to an art exhibition in 1917. He called it "*Fountain*" and signed it *R Mutt*.

By 1917, stodgy fine art was already under attack and *Marcel Duchamp* hammered another nail into its coffin. Yet stodgy fine art still lives, or maybe its a zombie?

The craziest thing about *Duchamp* declaring this *readymade* urinal to be art was that the art community bought it and art was irrevocably changed.

The urinal was photographed by *Alfred Stieglitz,* who is famous for working out that lines could transect the frame of a photograph (his photograph *Steerage*, for example).

Early photographers had not yet gotten their heads around this possibility. Studying art history lets you imitate the work of others (with your own spin) and still look cool and knowledgeable as you are *referencing* what has gone before.

Appropriation is a similar sort of copying but without giving credit, or the sort of credit that fellow artists who are in the know can read into your work if you are *referencing*.

Back to multiple images: When images are combined, their collective impact increases, unless you have an outstanding photograph that would be brought down by ordinary companions.

One example is *Eddie Adams'* photograph of *Nguyn Ngoc Loan,* executing a VC guerrilla on the streets of Saigon in 1968. *Nguyn* put a gun to the man's head and fired.

Eddie was there with his camera and the images made it onto mainstream media. We know killing still happens, but when is the last time it was shown on mainstream media?

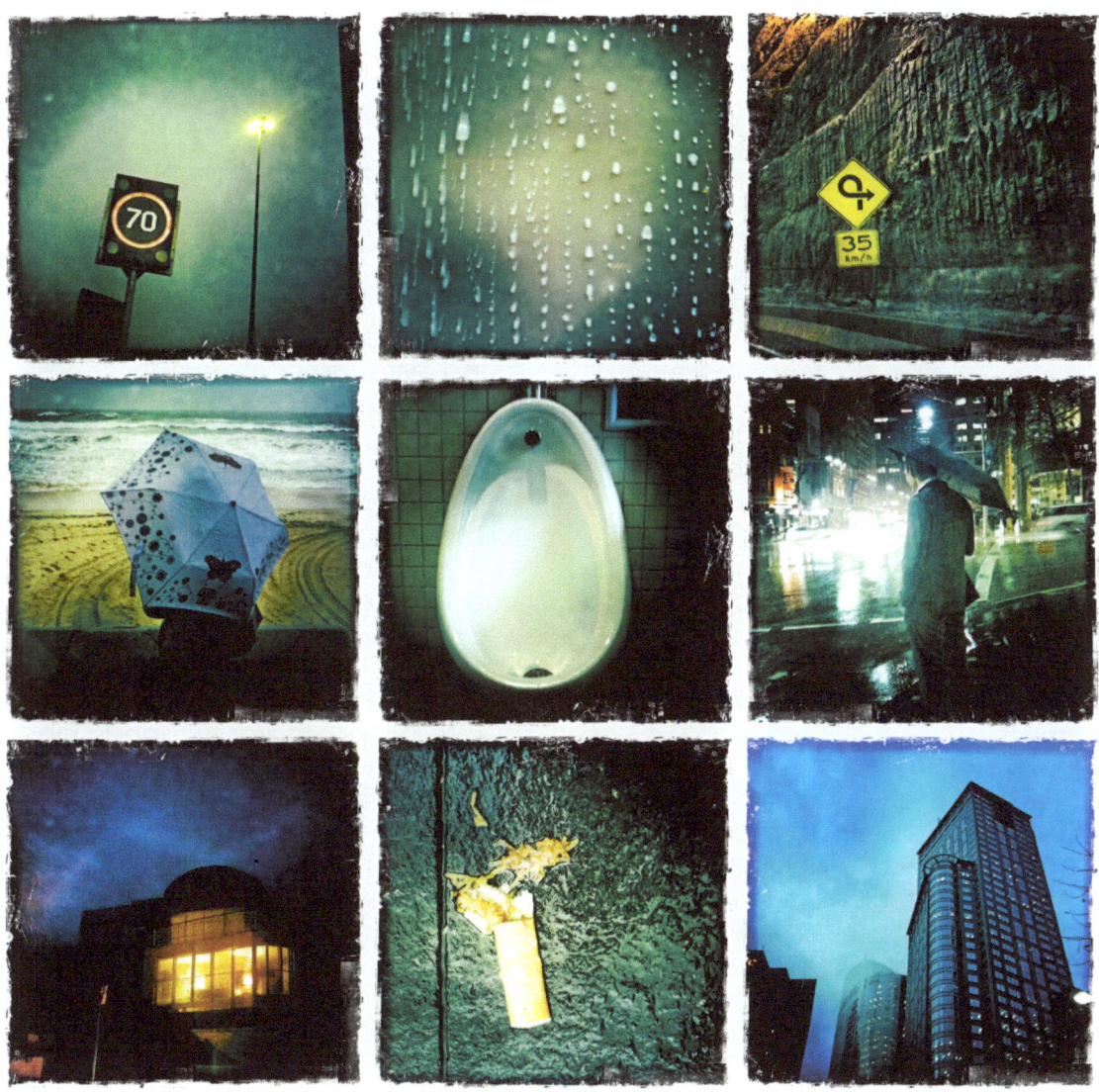

If you have "B Grade" images, put them together. Use *Photomontage*, create a design with them, or *Photoshop* them. Or do all three.

This may help. It may be fun, but it will be no substitute for having strong images in the first place. Every so often, however, *photomontage* does create magic.

Apart from a bunch of Germans and Russians in the early 20th Century, one of the world's most outstanding *Photomontagists* is a painter.

His name is *David Hockney*. He took many photographs, each of which did not amount to much. Then he combined them to try to make the camera record the world more as he saw it.

I watched a documentary on his work. I could see he was producing a stack of very average photographs. When he combined them, something amazing happened that I had not thought possible. He had created a new way of using a camera to see the world.

My 3x3 series are in part sailing on the breath of wind created by *David Hockney* in the 1980s.

But, as it turned out, one of my *iPhone* images said, "I want to stand by myself!"

I realised this when I showed my *Noughts and Crosses* series to a friend, with the comment that these images do not stand on their own, which is why I used the 3x3 array.

The response I got surprised me: "27A is fab, can't you see?" Yes, I was blind. 27A does have a lot of what makes a good photograph.

Looking at the image, I realised 27A was not *Robinson Crusoe*: I had created a photographic landscape crowded with low resolution, grainy, strangely coloured images, each of which stood on its own. Just differently to how I had thought it was necessary. Each image had a story to tell.

My smartphone photography had found its legs.

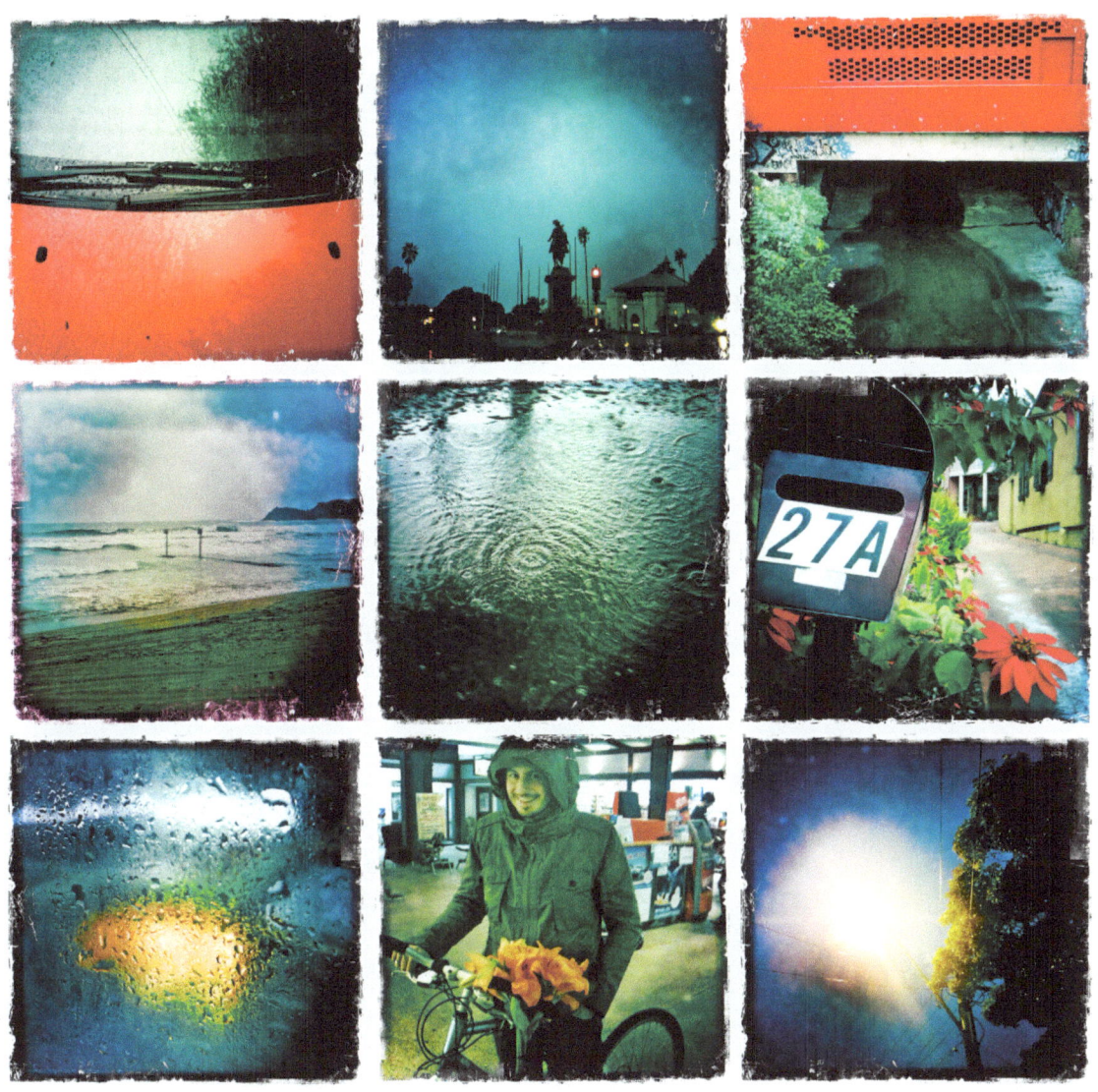

The *Bauhaus School* of the early 20th century revolutionised industrial design, architecture and more, as well as trying to identify fundamental building blocks of images.

In a similar way that words are derived from the letters a-b-c through to z, they looked for building blocks of images. Their answer:

> Circle
> Triangle
> Square

If you look at what the *Bauhaus* did, you will see why. They ignored fuzzy shapes and the patterns of nature. *Chaos Theory* was not yet invented so it didn't make it onto their canvas either.

The idea of these fundamental shapes works especially well in built environments. Here I have been looking into the gutter as opposed to the skies above, and noticed this fantastic triangle, pointing to the right.

Notice how the upper tip of the triangle nearly lines up with the reflection of the light pole? Noticing how things line up, or nearly don't, is crucial.

There is enough information in the reflections on the water to tell us this is a photograph. However, there is enough *abstraction* from the triangle in the foreground to create a healthy counterpoint.

Bauhaus theory didn't talk much about what one put inside these shapes or outside them for that matter. Thus, I was happy that I could add my own spin onto their rule without breaking it.

Nor did the *Bauhaus* elaborate much on what happened when circles, squares and triangles were put together to create complex shapes.

Lucky for you and me: we are saved from having to break the *Bauhaus* rules to get the photographs we want.

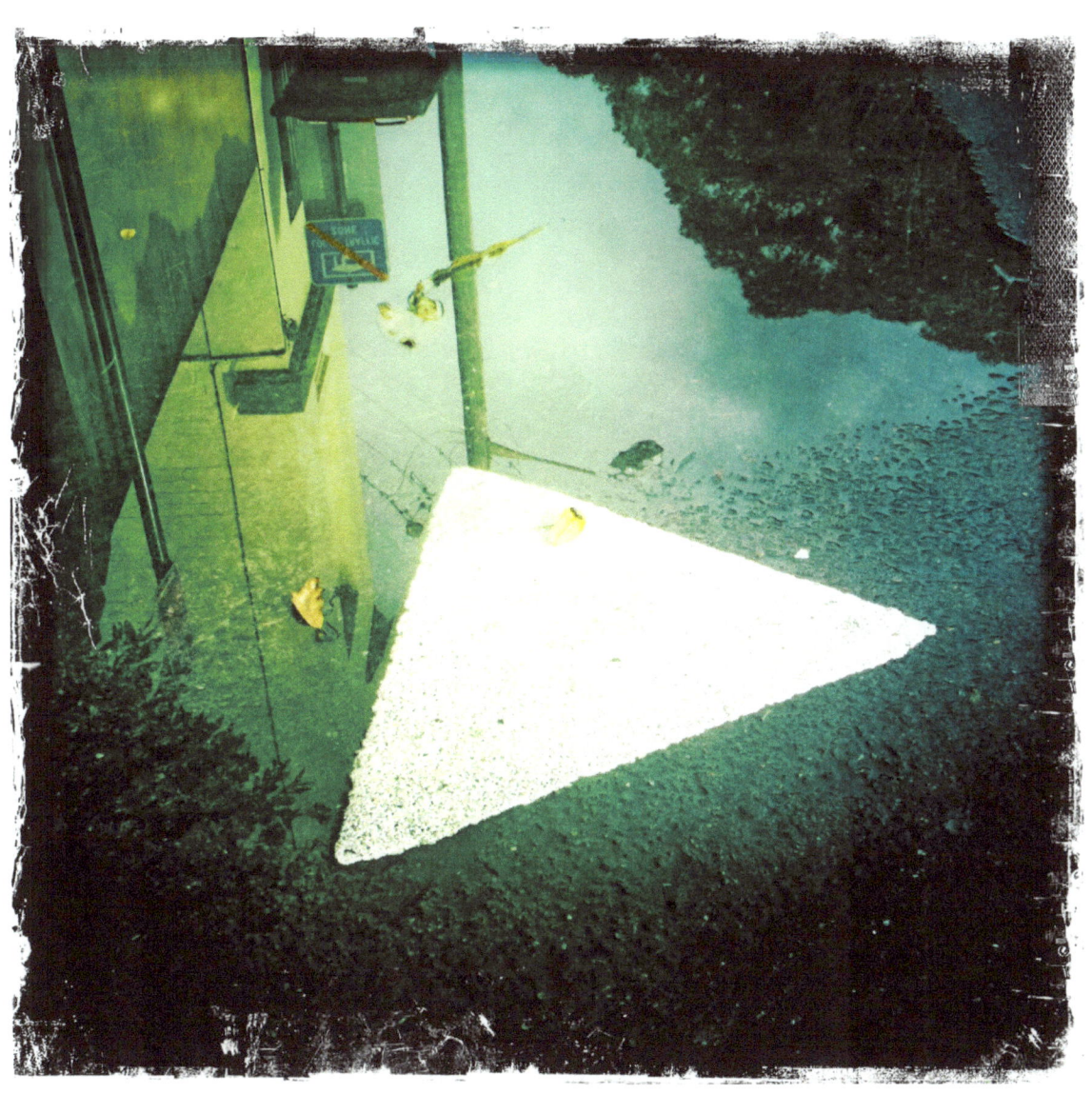

The image overleaf is a *Bauhaus* field day. All *the chickens have come home to roost.*

It's full of circles, triangles and squares, all in the one photo, and I didn't even have to cheat. Not to be disrespectful to those at the Bauhaus, let's say rectangles and squares are near enough to the same thing.

One commentator on the photo overleaf noted that the small rotation of the manhole cover really "fux with their mind".

In other words, there is a disturbing disjuncture. The diagonal yellow line has been thwarted in its attempt to cross the photograph unbroken.

One of the tricks I found with this sort of photography is to photograph things from straight on. Straight down in this case, or straight at a wall if that's the case.

This straightness gives an extra level of formality to the image. It ensures round things stay round and don't become ellipses.

Straightness in photos comes from using *F64* style cameras, such as the one I have when I'm paying homage to my photographic forefathers (page 2).

These cameras let you align and square up everything. They even have bubble levels to make sure everything is truly square, at least before you again bend it off level.

All photographs have edges. There is a real art to deciding where lines and shapes meet the edges of the photograph.

Notice how none of the lines land in the corners. If they had it would be an entirely different photograph.

Also the spokes of the manhole cover are a little bit off alignment to the edges of the photo. A bit of not quite straight in a photograph often works a treat.

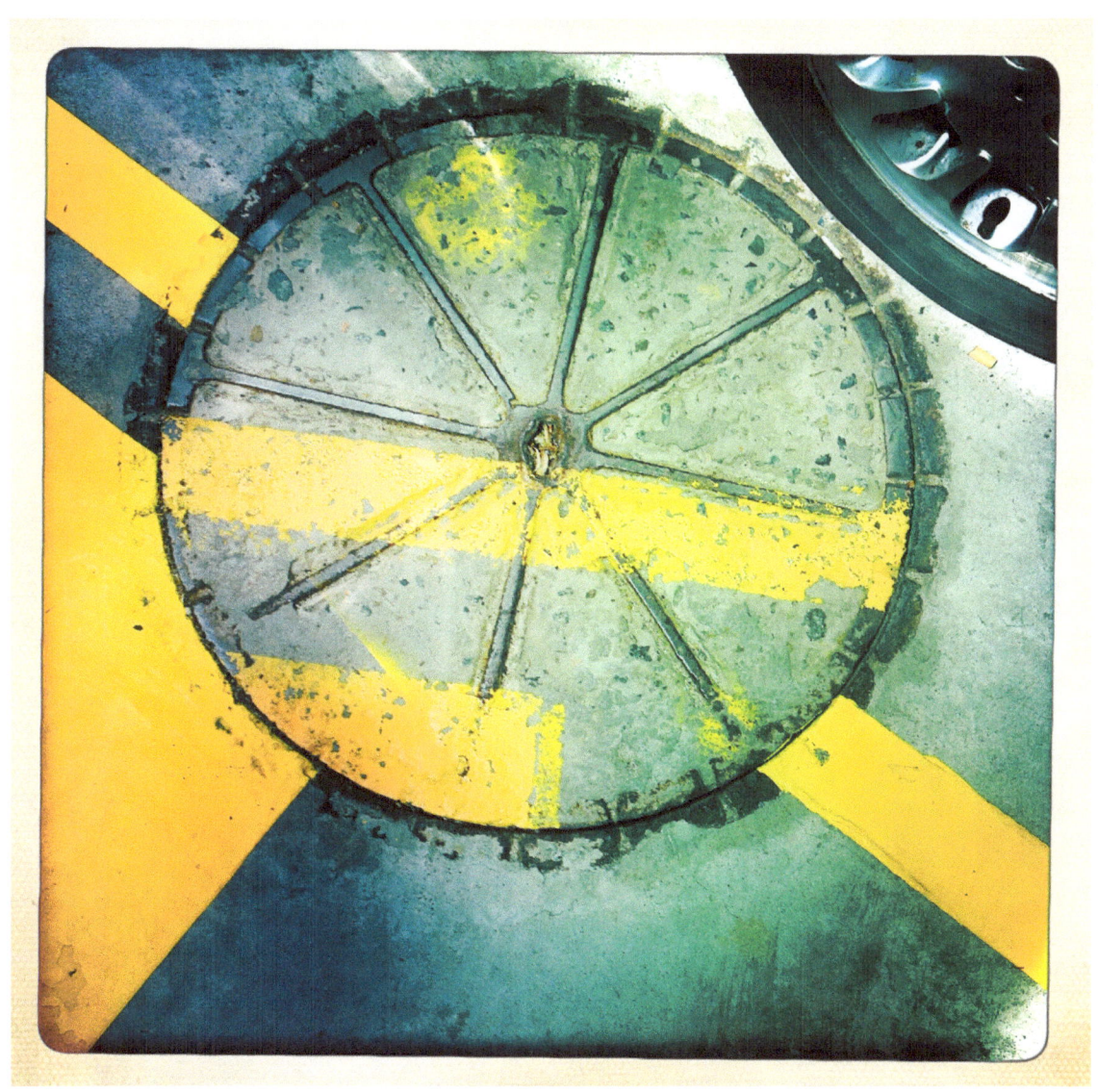

This is perhaps a good time to thank the *Bauhaus* for their achievements in *Modernism* and their well deserved place in history.

Modernism, after all, is such a good thing as it has given us *tubular steel chairs*, digital cameras, mobile telephones and *warming oceans*, but I digress.

Here we have peeling paint in an underground car park. The paint has peeled to reveal a *silhouette* of Buster the dog.

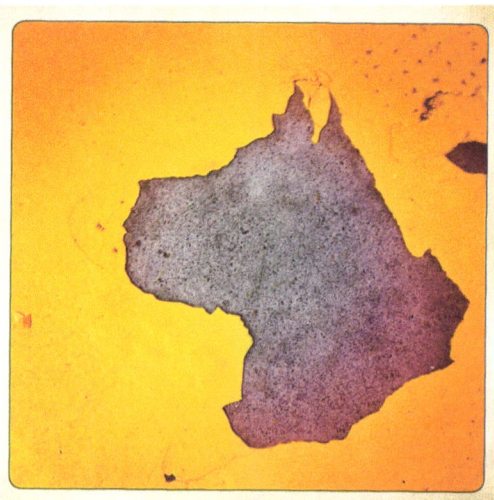

The passing cars (image right) have caused the paint to flake in an organic chaotic pattern. The early *modernists* didn't include chaos or the patterns of nature in their *visual vocabulary*. By contrast, the earlier *Art Noveau* movement cherished the patterns and intricacies of nature.

Interesting thing about patterns: if you can't see a *Pac Man*, raven, sitting dog and goat, you're not trying.

We have a tendency to see things we recognise, especially faces, even when as in this case, the car tyres never intended us to see faces.

Pareidolia is the word for recognising faces and objects in shapes. It happens to us all. Car designers deliberately give their cars faces and sometimes we photograph them with smartphones.

My imagination runs rampant, I can't help but think some cars now look like angry insects, swarming angrily through crowded city traffic.

While the *Bauhaus modernists* were doing their thing in Germany, in the 1920's, another German mucking around on a desk full of optical and watchmaking gear, hand built one of the world's most revolutionary cameras, the *Leica*.

This guy was called *Oskar Barnack*.

The beauty of his 1927 *Leica 1* was that it was small enough to be easily hand held, could easily be pointed in any direction, had great image quality, was very quiet and VERY FAST.

A generation earlier, cameras were like the one in the picture of me paying homage. This camera weighs 6kg and needs a tripod of similar weight to hold it. If I am fast, I can set up a shot in just under two minutes.

The *Leica* and others such as the *Contax*, gave rise to a generation of sneaks, people who wandered around taking photos of other people, often without them knowing.

The photographic genre of the *Decisive Moment* within the school of *Street Photography* was born.

Its core proposition: if anything is happening, one moment is better than all others in which to take a photograph. They called this the *Decisive Moment*.

If you are good, you will be ready with your camera before the *Decisive Moment* happens.

One of these *Leica* cameras crossed the border into France and landed in the hands of one *Henri Cartier-Bresson*. This guy was amazing. I read he had the ability to wander around the streets with a *Leica* glued to his face without being noticed.

Many of his photographs are taken without the awareness or any prior permission of his subjects.

He also photographed landscapes, but I doubt he ever asked them for permission. I don't think anyone ever has, nor has anyone ever paid royalties to a landscape.

The photographs right and on the following pages show that the spirit of *Henri Cartier-Bresson* still lives and people still *jump puddles*.

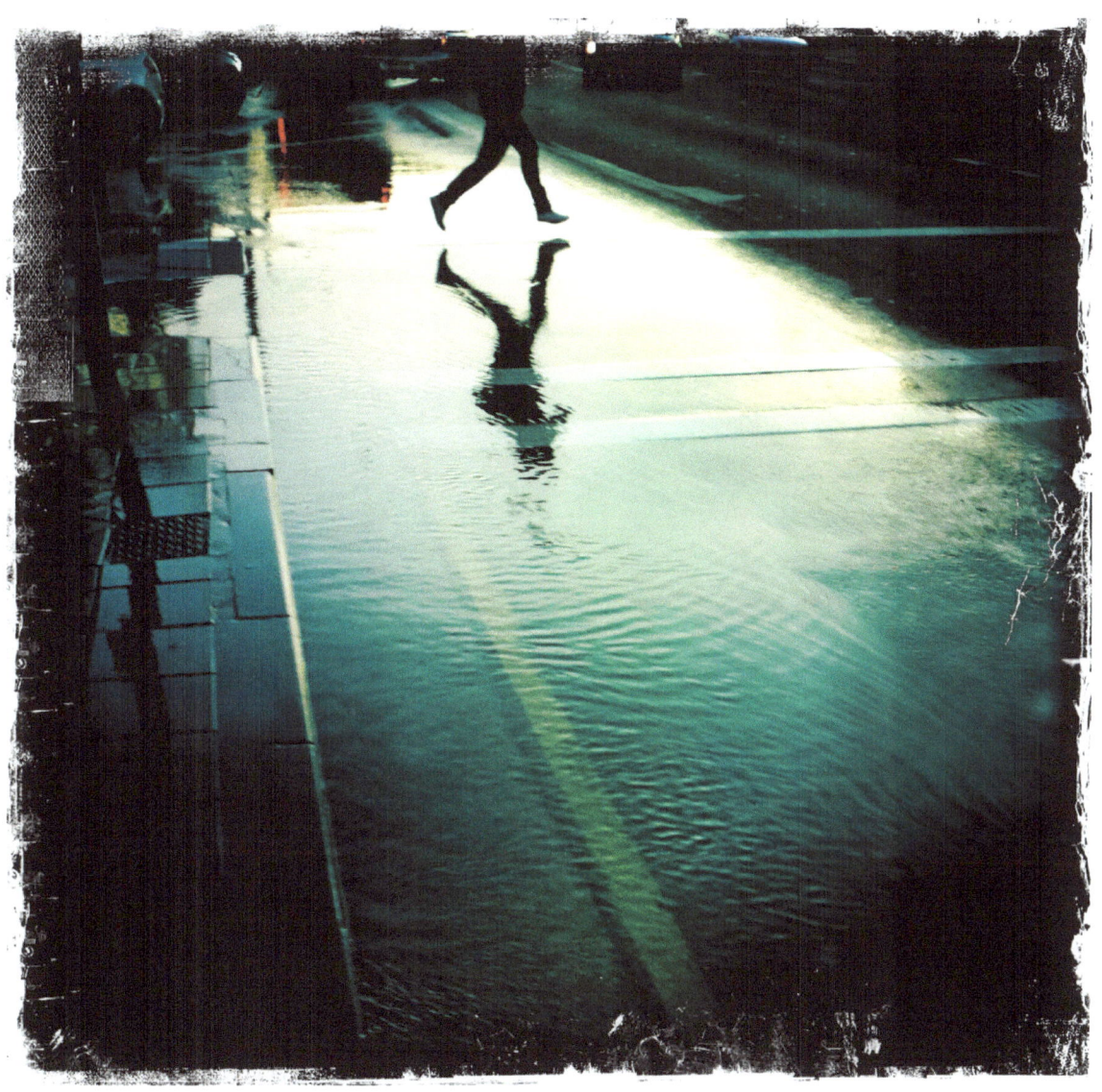

On this crowded street, most people had a smartphone, but no one else saw this photographic opportunity. Had they studied *Henri Cartier-Bresson*, I would have had to jostle for the shot like a press photographer. Instead, I had it all to myself.

A great way of finding photographic opportunities is to look at what others have seen before and then build your own vision on top of that. By the time you are done, it will be uniquely yours too, not a copy or an imitation.

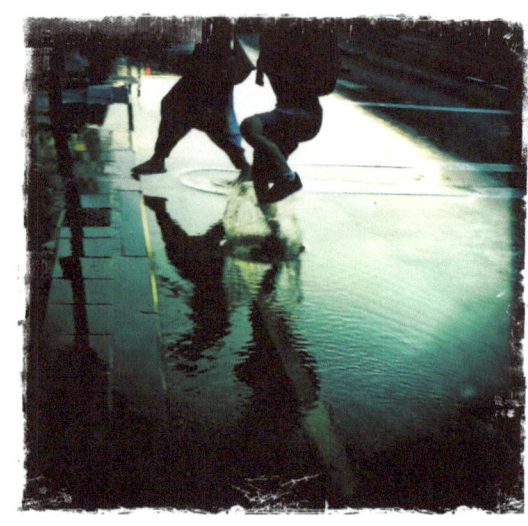

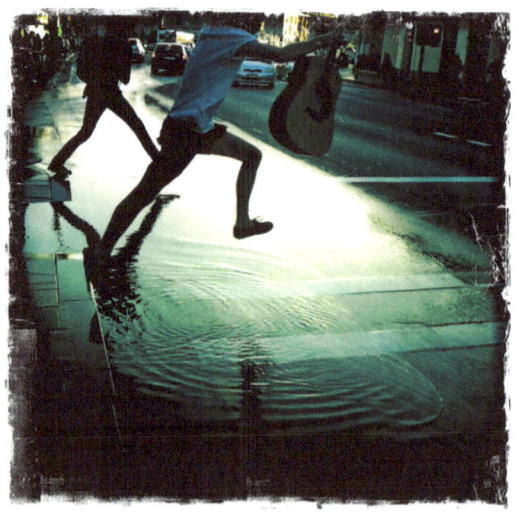

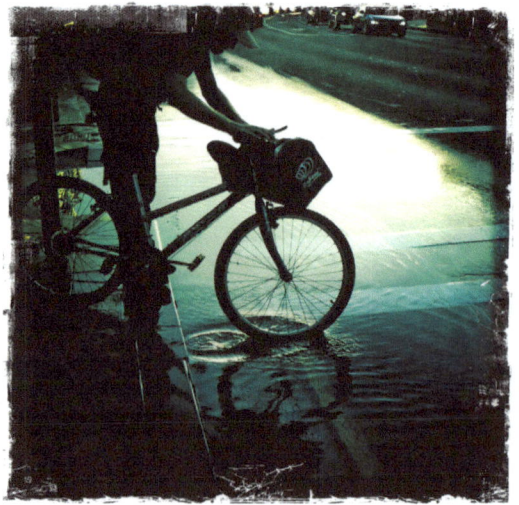

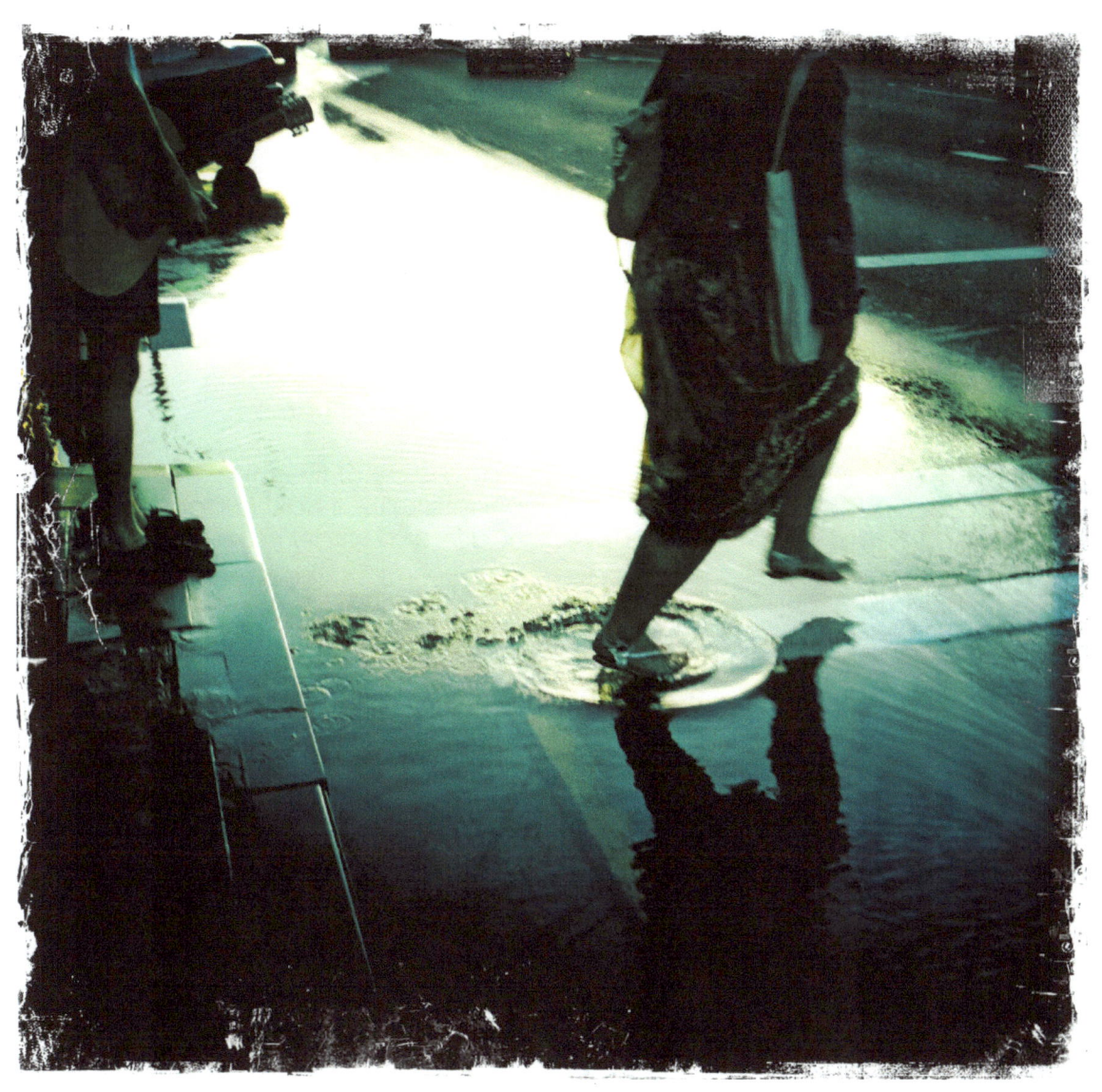

It is very cold, *raining cats and dogs*, and evening rush hour. I see this delightful young man (whom I have not met before nor since) with flowers and clearly on a mission to please someone.

I ask him if I can take a photograph, he agrees and then I email him a copy, on the spot. For all its glory, the *Leica* could not do that.

I generally like to photograph people with their permission, if not in advance, then by checking with them after taking the photograph.

The issue of the right to photograph anyone on the street is interesting. Much hot air is expelled by both camps. There is confusing legislation and unclear case history on this subject.

The other issue that attracts a lot of discussion is whether a photograph is real photojournalism or a setup. The man right could be a friend of mine and the photograph entirely a setup.

This is nothing new. One of the most disputed photographs ever is *Robert Capa's 1936 Death of a Loyalist Soldier*. Its legitimacy is disputed to this day.

Later *Capa* used a German camera similar to a *Leica*, a *Zeiss Contax II* to photograph for American Magazines while America was at war with Germany.

Never let politics get in the way of using the best camera.

Capa did not live long. Being a war photographer has its occupational health and safety issues.

One advantage of photographing charming young men with flowers is the photographer is much more likely to have a long life.

Charming young men with flowers are also much more likely to have a long life than their gun carrying counterparts.

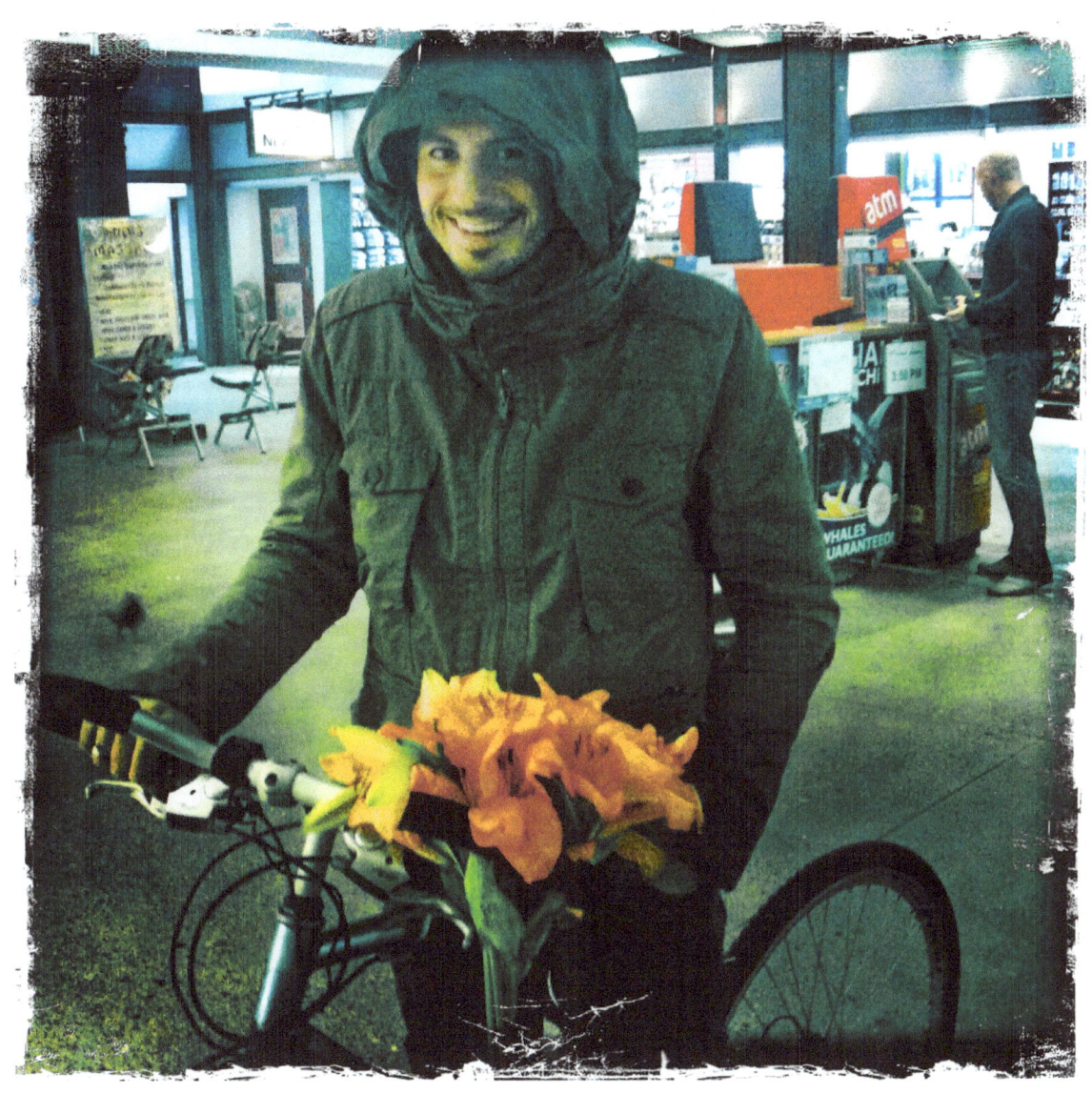

Joel Meyerowitz was one of the first American street photographers to use colour in the 1960s. At that time, many thought proper photography was *Black and White*. Colour was for amateur holiday snaps.

In the BBC series *The Genius of Photography*, *Joel* said his *street photography* was sometimes like a baseball fielder catching a ball. His job was to capture some random or quirky moment, using his camera as a photographic equivalent of a baseball glove.

I am catching such a photographic ball (image opposite). It's the festive season in the city and the man with the oversized carrot is clearly out to communicate the hazards of overdoing it with the vegetables at diner. I was sitting down at a café and didn't even need get off my chair to get the shot.

I also didn't get around to asking anyone for permission (nor in the photograph right), It doesn't work readily with this sort of photography.

The law and rights of a photographer are on my side in these cases. If I were to do something silly like making it look like the photographed person is endorsing something and use the photograph in an advertising campaign, I would be living very dangerously, especially if the person was a celebrity with a lawyer.

Many people go to third world countries for their *street photography*, as there are fewer legal limitations on photographers and fewer legal remedies for people being photographed.

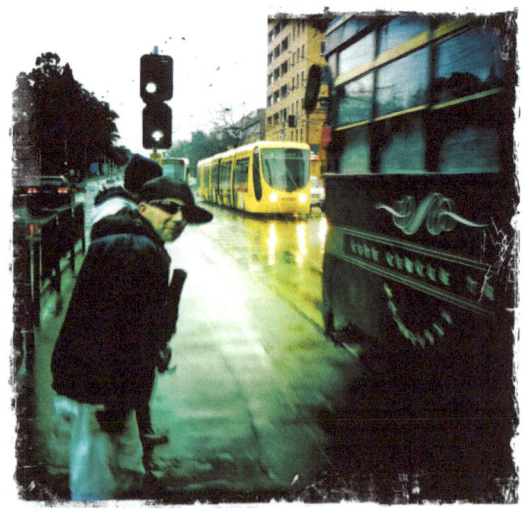

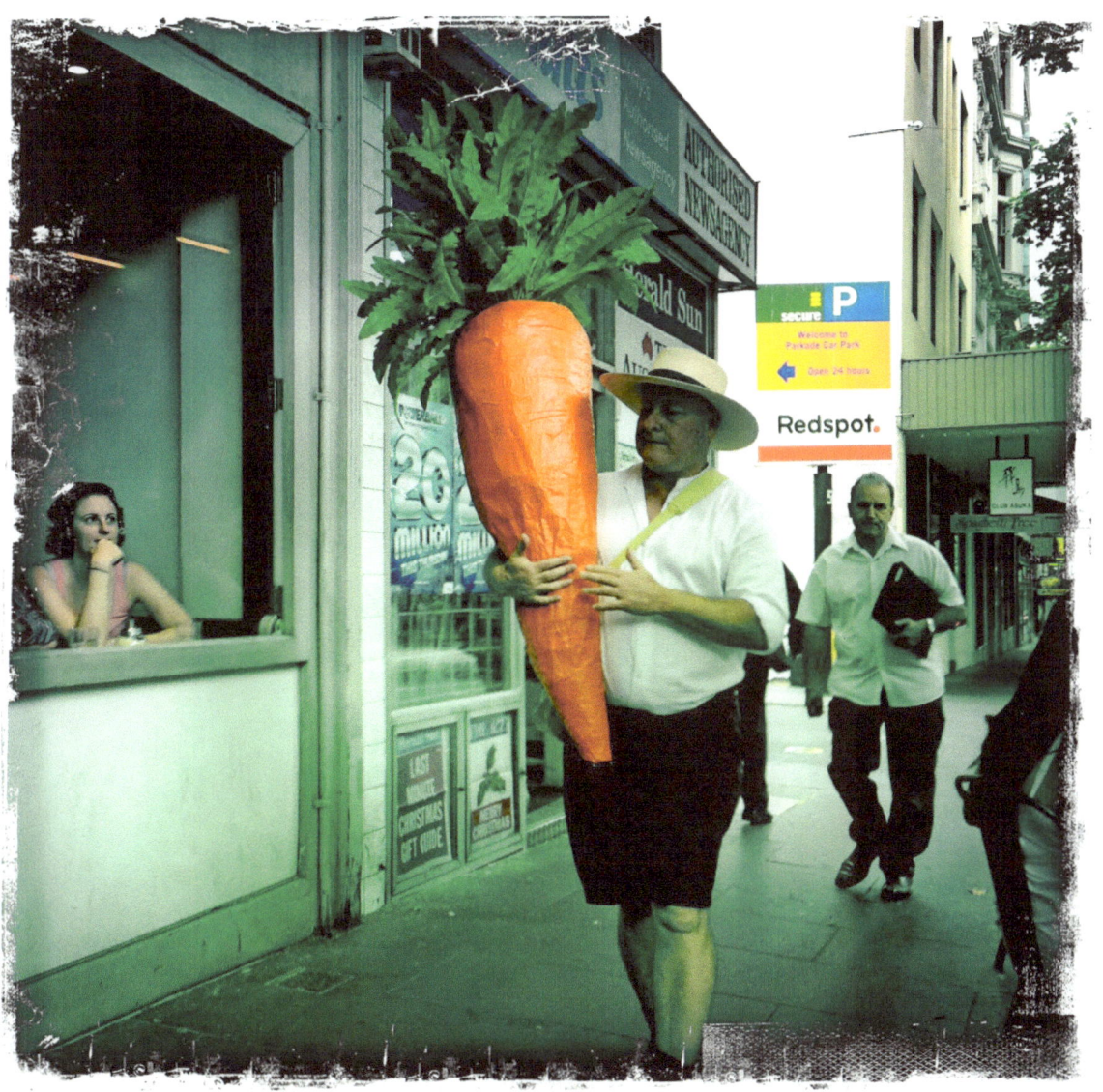

On the street or travelling, we are presented with a feast of images and occurrences. In all cases, there is a story, a *narrative*.

Sometimes the story is a simple pleasure such as running through a buried tyre at the beach, or a sense of weariness in a hard-edged city.

Whatever might have been in the mind of the photographer or the people being photographed, it is in the nature of photography that the viewer will always supply their own interpretation.

A friend provided a commentary to the photograph right:

> "...you capture moving moments in people's lives and their places - the clocks, the texting girl sheltering from the rain, the bikes fallen on the wet footpath and that SUV appearing to be waiting for someone to arrive on platform 23. Have you read *Sebald's Austerlitz*? I could write a book like that with photos like this one."

My initial response: "*Sebald* who? and what am I missing out on?"

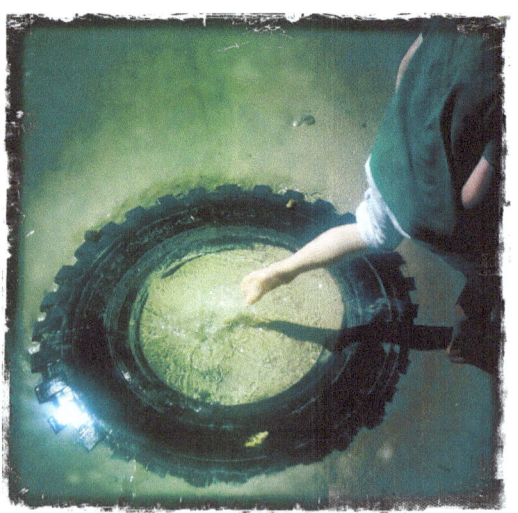

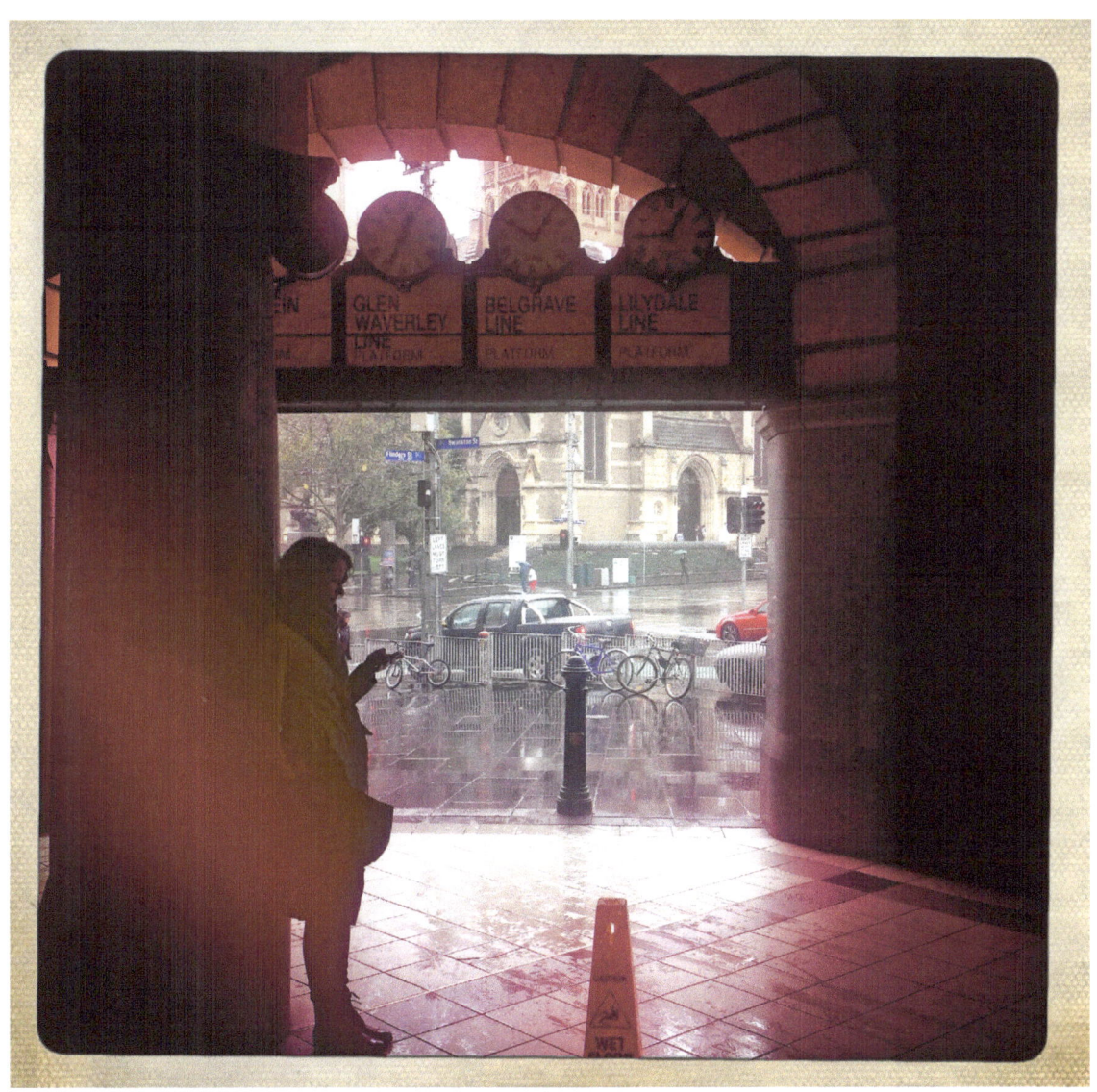

5

Photography's Brush Strokes

The *Decisive Moment* is about finding the one moment in the flux of time when all aspects of an image come together and it really sings.

Sometimes this is clear and sometimes it's not. It's a case-by-case thing. What is remarkable is how a photograph grabs a segment of time, and how much the message of a photograph can change from one frame in a sequence to the next.

Each art form has its own language created by the media it uses.

If you are a painter, you will see the effect of the canvas, brush marks, smears, bristles stuck in the paint and so on. If you are *Jackson Pollock*, tracks left by the tricycle you rode over the wet canvas will be integral to your artistic medium.

When things get dark, the *iPhone* struggles, the early ones especially, as in this sequence. *Exposure* times increase and things get blurry from the subject's or the photographer's movement, or both. *Image noise* or *grain* makes an appearance.

Photography has its own language of *grain*, or its complete absence and freezing motion, or blurring it.

Digital image noise is a bit like *film grain* and is usually unwanted, along with blur, unless they work creatively. Then we hit gold.

The crazy thing about photography is that what can kill one photograph saves another. There are few, if any, concrete rules.

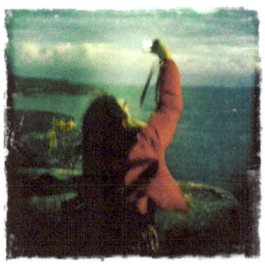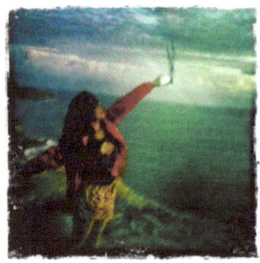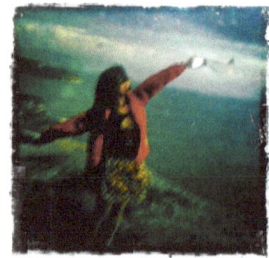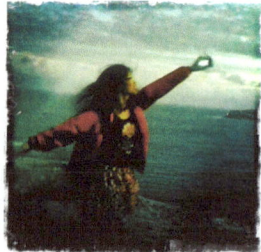

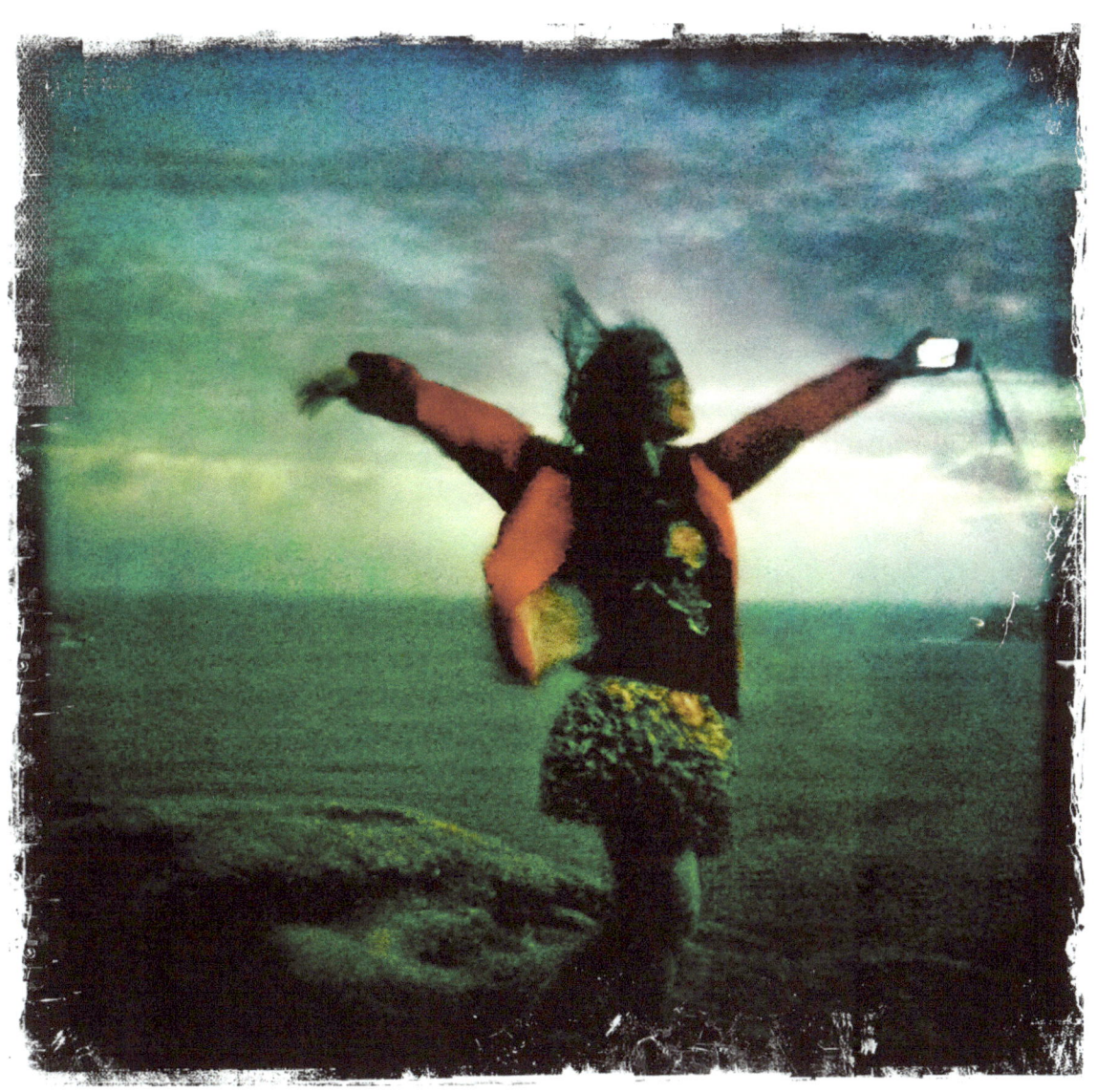

6

If you have never done this, you have never played. Stamp your foot hard onto a puddle, lake or ocean. If it's not raining, create a puddle or go somewhere where there is water and DO IT! Bring your camera.

Remember I said the *Leica* was FAST.

If you know how to use a *Leica*, you will set up the camera before the shot. This means you will decide on film, *ISO (formerly ASA or DIN)*, film development chemistry, temperature and time, you will select a *shutter speed*, an *aperture*, and you will *pre-focus* before the shot.

Used this way even a *1954 Leica M3* beats ALL CURRENT digital cameras with its 16 millisecond *Shutter Lag*.

Shutter Lag is the delay between when you press the *shutter* and when the *exposure* starts.

Current pro-DSLR cameras lag about 40 milliseconds. Cheap consumer cameras and some smartphones lag enough to read *War and Peace* before the photograph starts.

How did I get the timing of the splash with an older laggy *iPhone*?

The answer: I press the *shutter button* to take a photograph of what has not yet happened. This is *photographic anticipation*. Meaning I had a sense of the *shutter lag* and photographed ahead of time to get the shot.

If you see an image in the camera viewfinder you will never be able to photograph it. It has gone forever. Your reaction time will be 120 milliseconds if you are amongst the fastest humans. Typically, it will be twice that. Then your camera adds to this delay.

The iPhone 6s reduced *shutter lag* with a trick called *Live Photos*. It rapidly takes and discards photos, except for one, the moment you press the button.

Photographic anticipation is your saviour. It's like drummers anticipating the beat of the rhythm rather trying to hit the drum once they have heard the beat. Practice it. Develop your sense of timing so that you take photographs that you expect will happen.

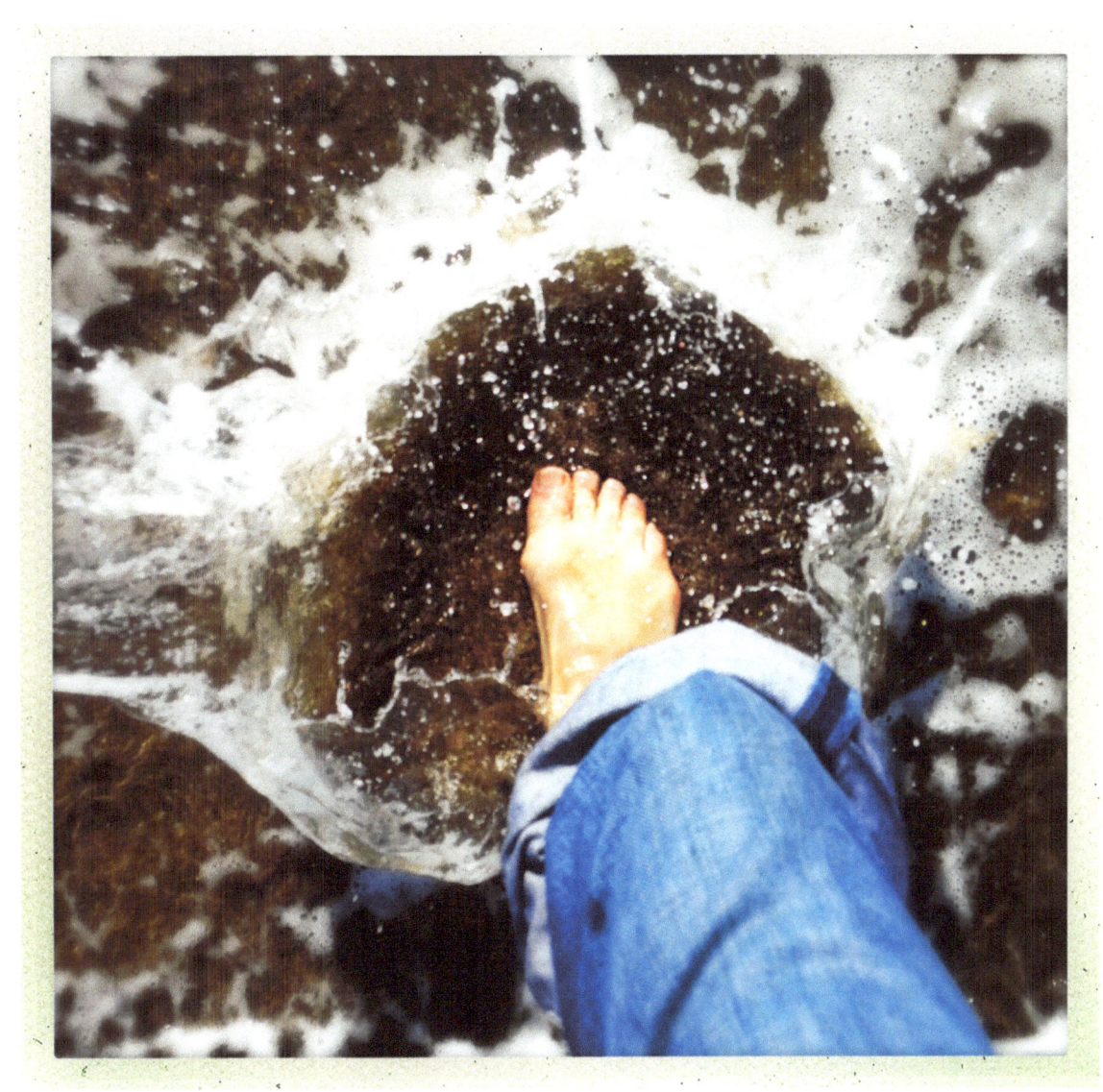

I find pavement endlessly interesting. It's crowded and littered with *unintentional art*.

My greatest challenge is noticing when this makes a photograph, and when boring pavement is just boring pavement.

Ernst Haas was one of the earlier post WWII colour photographers to examine pavement with a camera. One of his photographs is a *Tin Can Buddha**, a car crushed can that takes on the appearance of a sitting Buddha.

This type of tin can is no longer made so I have no chance of copying him.

Another find is a spill that looks like an ad for anti-acid medication.

My favourite is the coffee cup car park road kill which tells the story of its very messy demise.

What I like is how the splatter contrasts the clean formalism of the cup itself. It looks as if the cup has come from a formally lit product shot or an artists illustration.

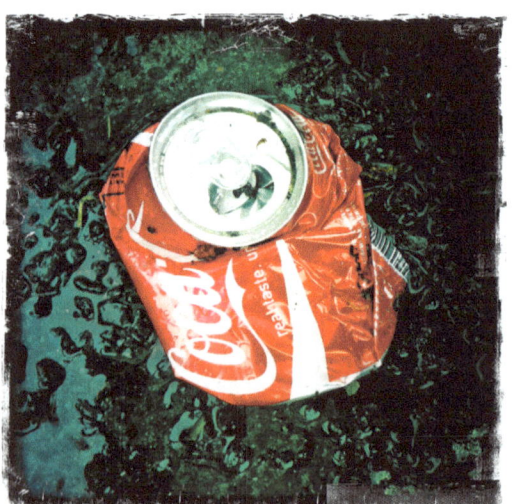

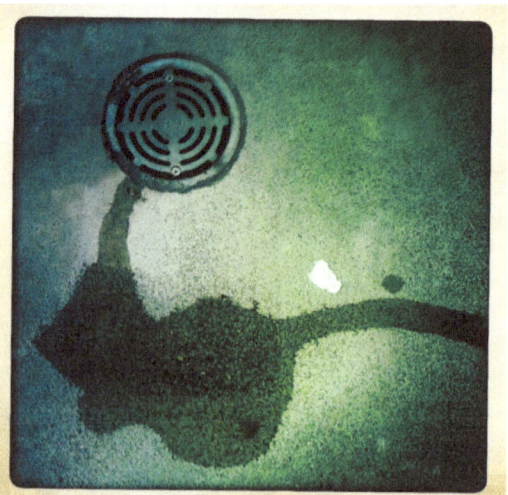

* this photograph takes some finding

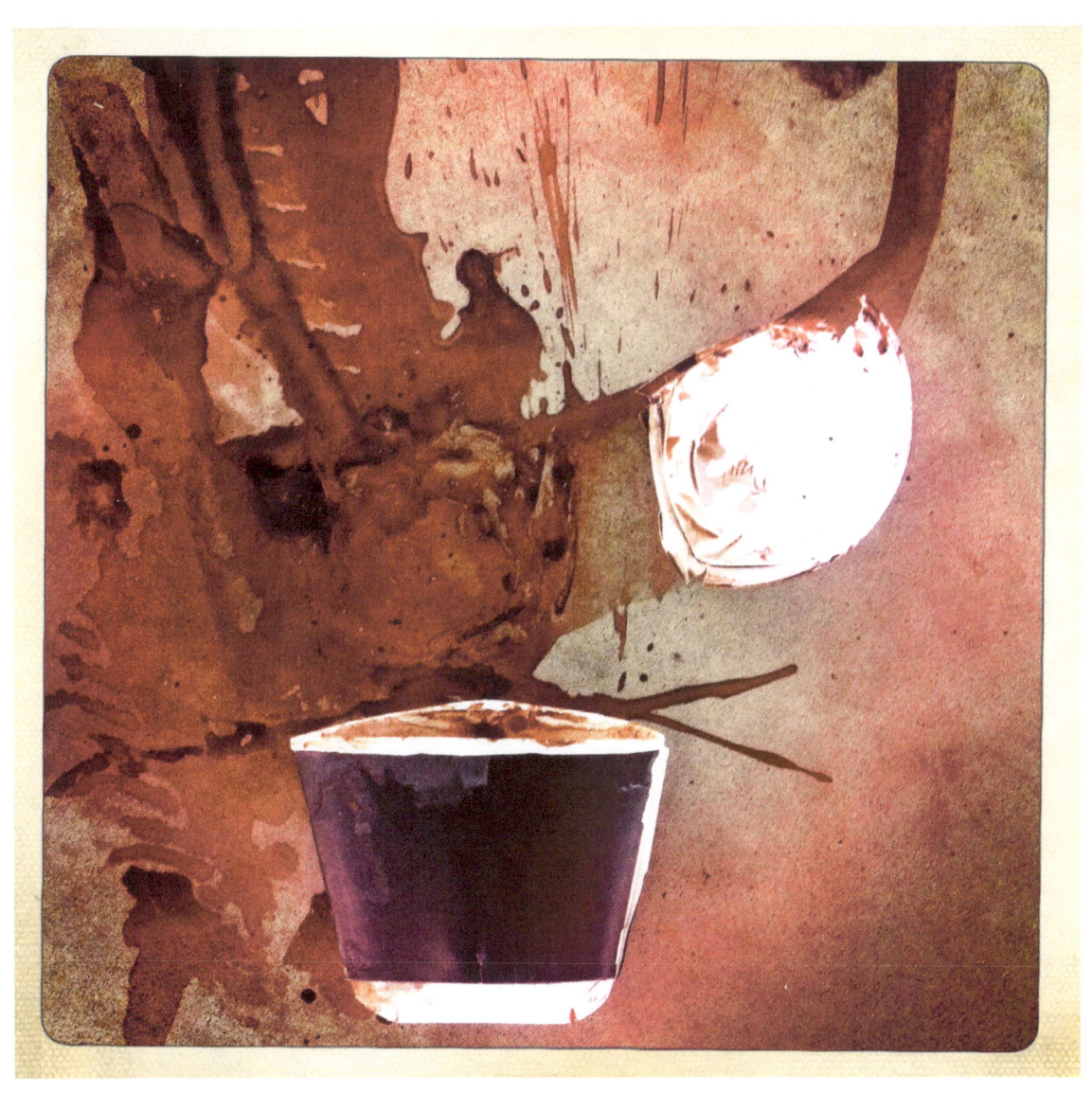

Another fascinating thing is liquid spills. They are such a rich photographic lode and often visited by a good friend of ours: *Pareidolia*.

Car tyres have created a Chinese Dragon below and the spill right is a shoot-'em-up character from a crazy western movie. You will have to believe me that these two images are as found. I did not work them with a paint brush.

There is a saying that one should not *cry over spilt milk*. Overleaf is a photograph of my feet on the gutter, with a spectacular view of *spilt milk*. It was not my milk, so I felt only a compulsion to photograph it.

I was fascinated by the illusion of depth created, as if there were the vast open universe of space, a *Milky Way*, just beneath my feet.

With photography, a well-developed metaphorically oriented imagination will serve you well.

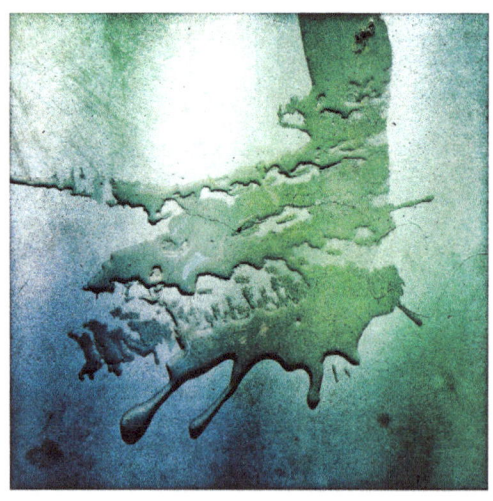

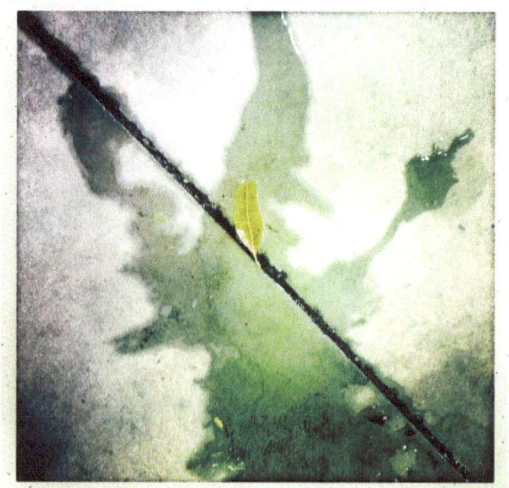

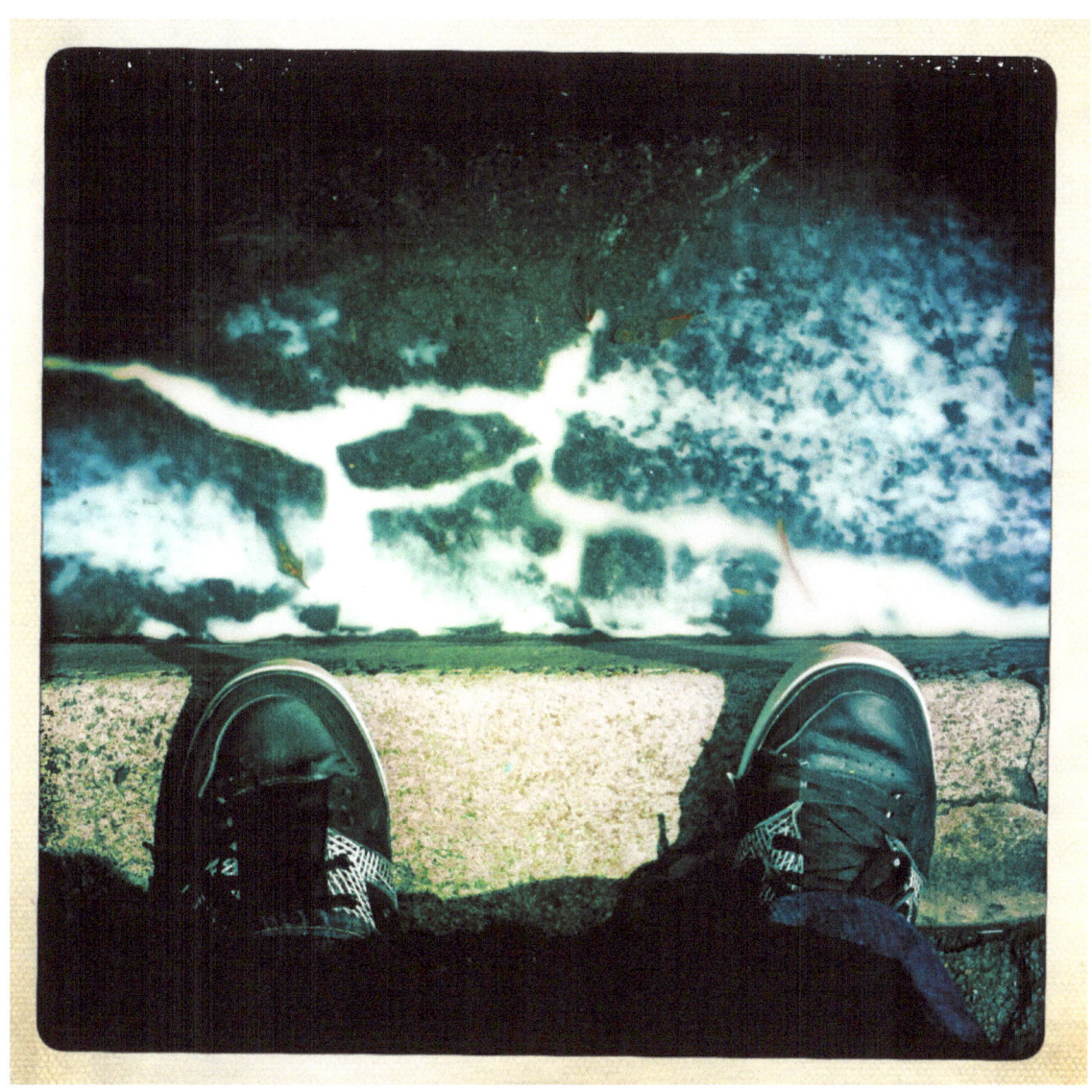

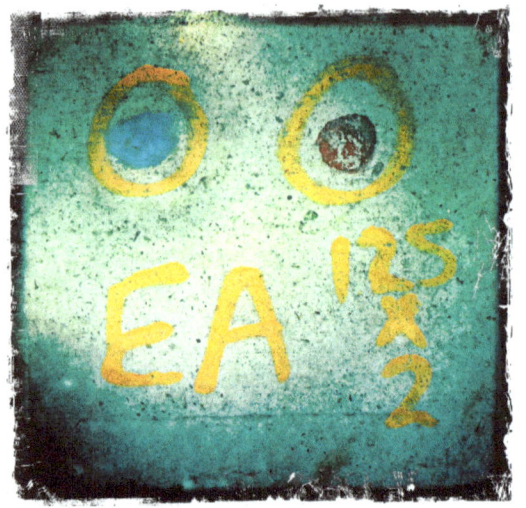

In many cities, government-paid graffiti artists paint lines, letters and numbers on the pavement when they find a pipe or cable under the ground. I declare this to be *found art*, a relative of the *readymades*.

The contemporary movement of *Stuckism* is in part a reaction against these movements. It is not a reversion to *classicism*, but an insistence that skill on the part of the artist is required.

Right: skill on the part of a littering artist, if not an an artistic work, gives these birds a free lunch.

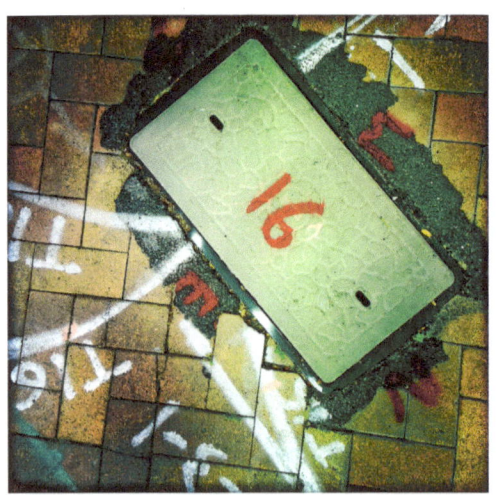

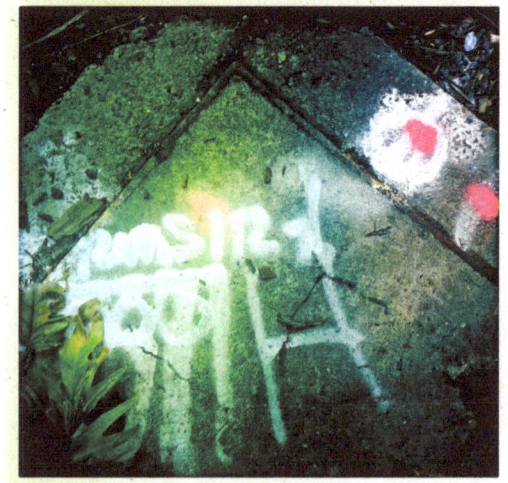

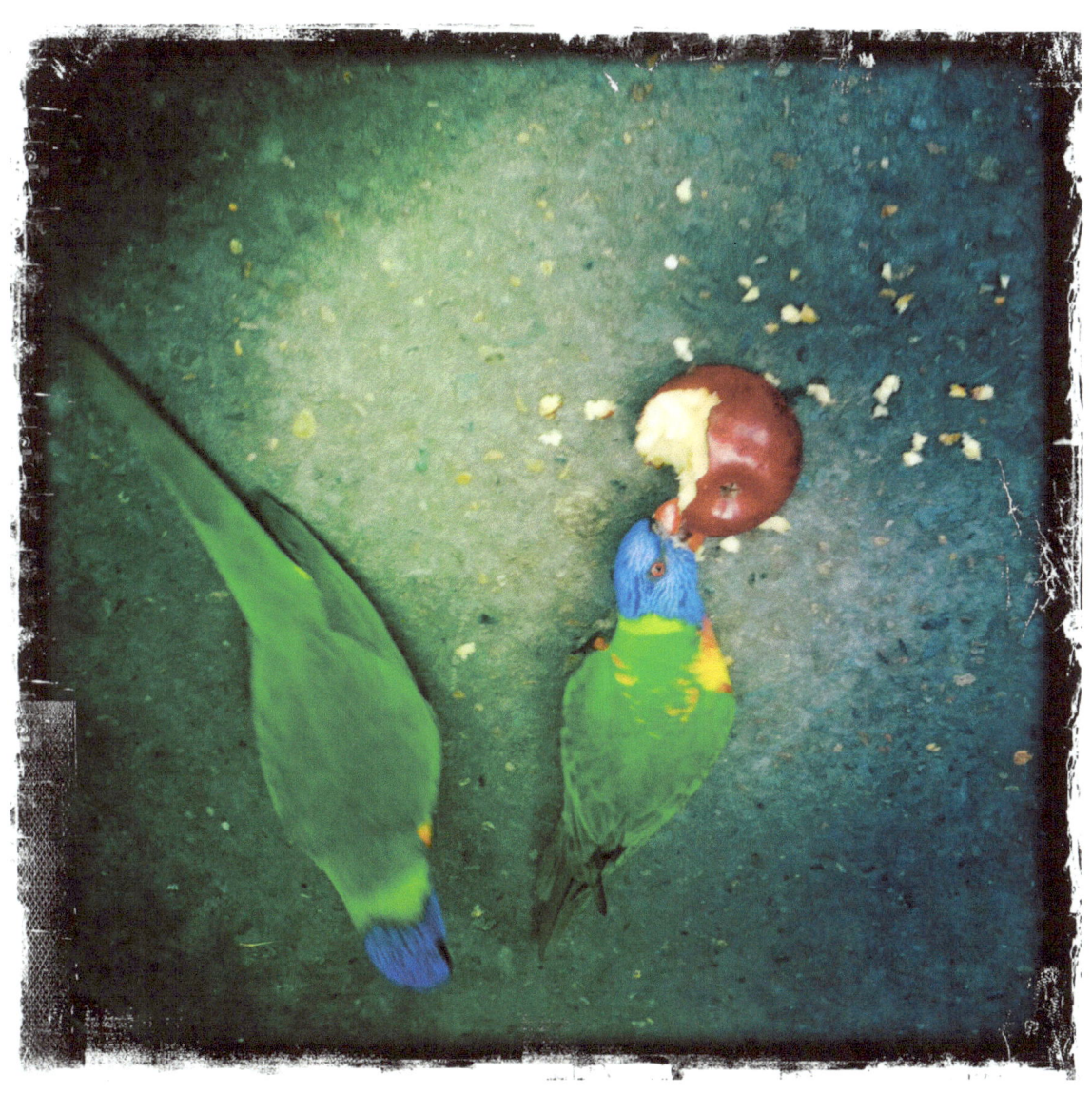

7

Digital Asset Management

Digital Asset Management (DAM) is all about making sure your digital photographs can be found when you look for them and importantly also, are not degraded.

DAM is photography geek-speak for backing up and organising your photographs.

There was a great image I was going to show you on the opposite page.

A motor scooter is parked in a disabled car park and the painted person on the wheelchair graphic on the wall lines up to the handlebars of the scooter and mimics its form. The pastel greenish colours of the scooter really work well against the yellow painted graphic on the blank concrete wall of the carpark.

It is a great *juxtaposition* and a dire warning about the consequences of not being a safe scooter rider.

Unfortunately, I lost the image so you will just have to take my word for it.

This page has been Unintentionally left Blank.

Dirt and finger grease and perhaps the remnants of that last tofu burger you ate WILL accumulate on the lens of your smart phone.

One discourse I read on the subject asserted that dirt on the lens was a major limitation to the sharpness of smartphone cameras.

Sometimes dirt or grease look like a haze that resembles the *soft focus* treatment that was popular ages ago. Sometimes they just destroy the image. Here is a trick: deliberately smear the lens to create an effect.

In the "olden days", photographers put *Vaseline* (petroleum jelly) onto a screw on filter over the lens. I tried it and ended up with a blurry mess. There was an art to using *Vaseline* that has been lost and not found, at least by myself.

The image overleaf has the perfect amount of Chinese lunch on the lens to create the right amount of softness without losing important image detail. The softness is really a haze that shows up most strongly around highlights, *specular* ones especially, such as the sun shining off the metal rail.

The better filters that were popular in film photography days were much more sophisticated than dirt or grease. They overlaid two images, one sharp and one hazy. Some camera makers made special *soft focus* portrait lenses by which the level of *soft focus* was adjustable.

Hasselblad had, and I think still has, soft focus filters, the *Softar I, II & III*.

Years ago I worked for a portrait studio where the *Softar III* was used for everything except the before shots, which also got lighting that was guaranteed to make anyone look horrid.

The photos were so soft that the retouch artist (pre-digital, using a fine paintbrush) had to paint details back into the photograph, such as the iris of the person's eye. I didn't last long there.

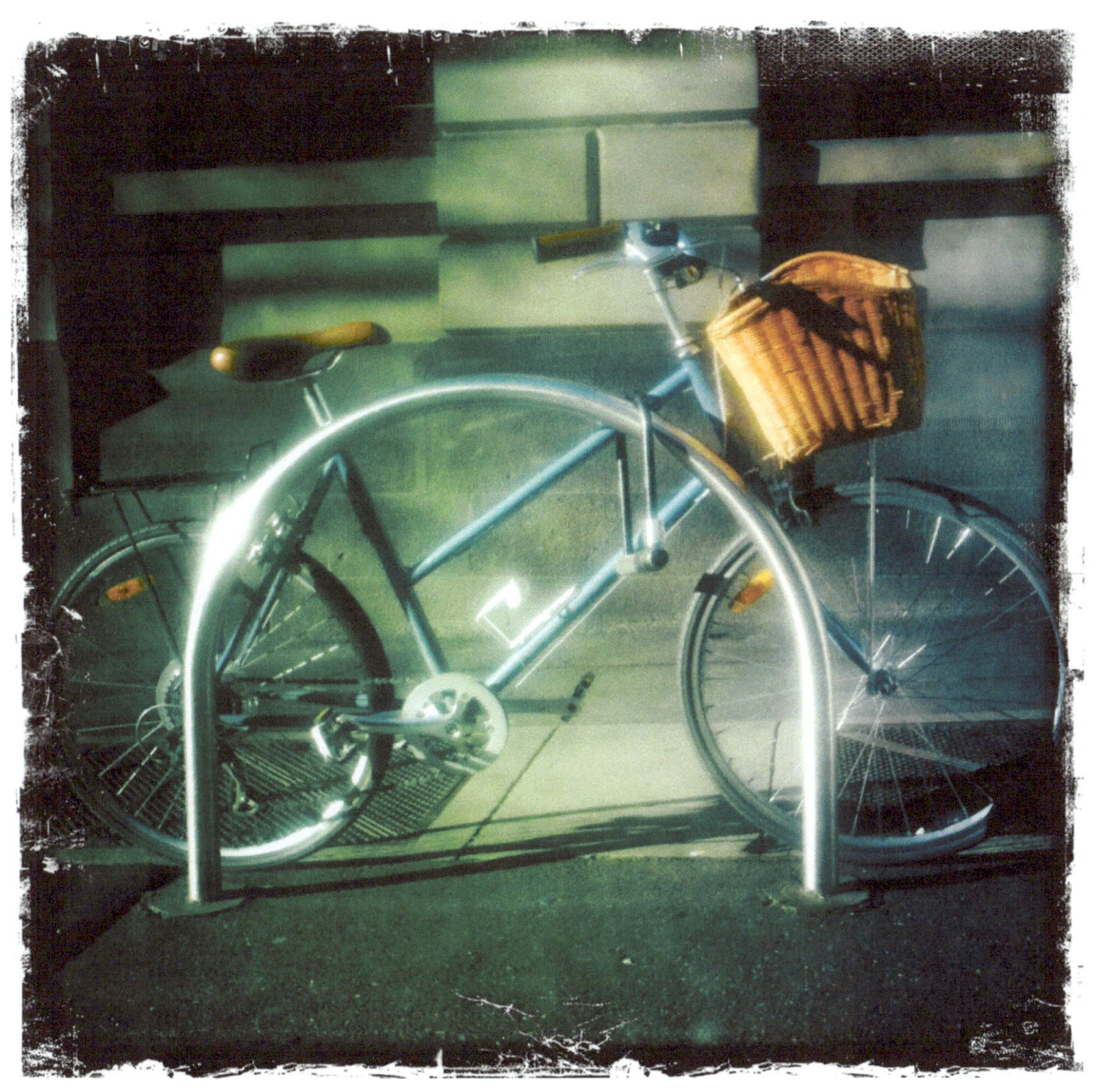

I smeared the lens of my smart-phone with a diagonal swipe of a greasy finger and took photos. I experimented until I got one I liked.

Lesson: the angle of the smear equals the angle of the *star-burst* (there still are *star-burst* filters). There is just the right amount of grease on the lens overleaf and below. Experiment!

To give equal time to an alternative view in photography education, I am obliged to include the following, even though it is not corroborated by science:

> The starburst in the photo overleaf is proof that aliens visit the earth in star ships that fly close to the sun (so we can't see them) but result in star-bursts that are evident in the photos of certain smart phones in certain conditions.

A crazy thing about *iPhones* is their *shutter speed*. It can get VERY HIGH. The photograph overleaf has the highest *shutter speed* (shortest duration) of any of my photographs ever: 1/21,000 second.

My Pro-DSLR maxes out at 1/8,000 second, though if I am cunning with a *flash*, I can get shorter *exposure* times but only in darkness.

Check out the work of *Harold "Doc" Edgerton*. He pioneered high speed *stroboscopic photography*. Every time you use a camera *flash*, you are walking in his footsteps.

The photo below was of the moon. It looks like the sun but the *exposure* is 1/15 second. Photographically, the moon is very much like the sun, just 400,000 times darker.

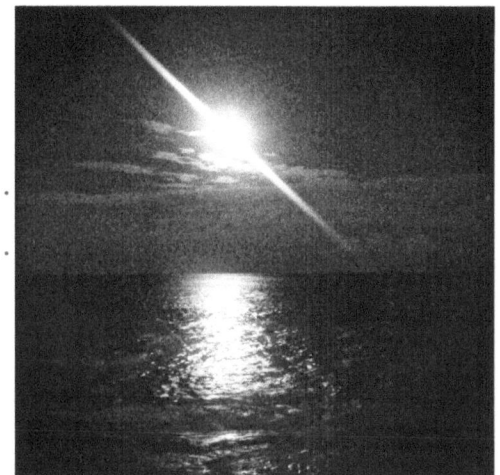

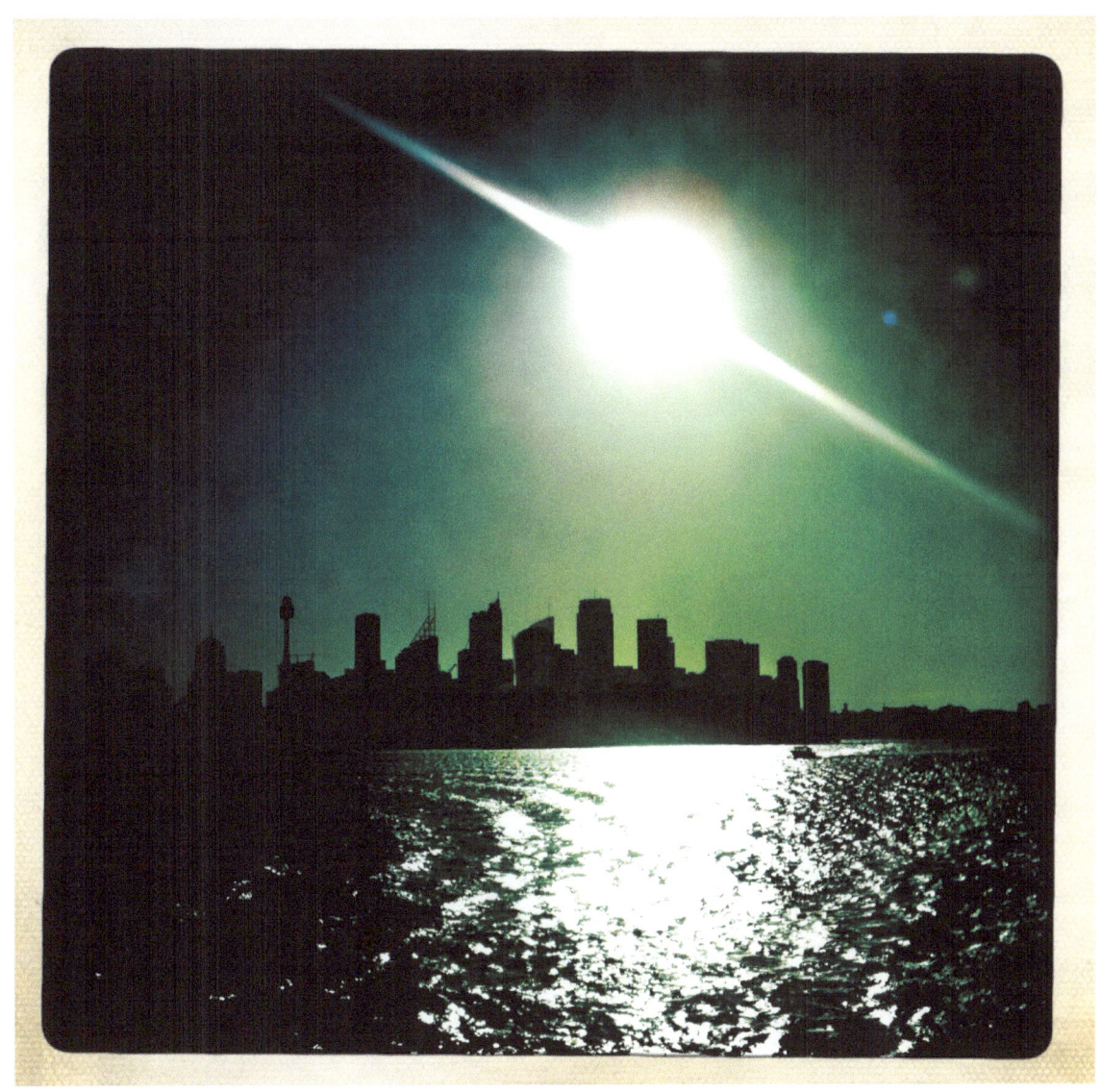

Colour

To me, this lichen covered rock resembles a shy fish. I also really like its colour and that of the surrounding vegetation. Orange and green work well together.

Colour and its effect on our response to light and images is a huge subject, the understanding of which is rapidly developing.

You will find well developed "rules" in art circles about which colours go with other colours, and which don't.

Colour has a large impact on how we perceive images, our environment, ourselves and others. It contributes substantially to the emotional impact of our visual sense.

While researching this subject, I found *The Manchester Colour Wheel*.

A group of scientists (from guess where?) got people to undertake a *UK Mental Health Questionnaire* that tests for one of three mental states:

Normal: Anxious: Depressed.

The same people were then asked to choose colours. The results are not surprising: depressed people chose depressing colours, happy people chose happy colours, anxious people were somewhere in between.

Picasso was a master of depressive colour during his *Blue Period*.

The Manchester research was so definitive that it is possible to predict how people would perform on the *UK Mental Health Questionnaire* by their colour choice.

Skip the tedious questionnaire and just pick a few colours and your doctor will know if you need to be prescribed *Prozac* or maybe exercise, a good diet and some uplifting cognitive therapy.

Based on the Manchester results, the rock that looks like a fish may be anxious but probably does not need *Prozac*.

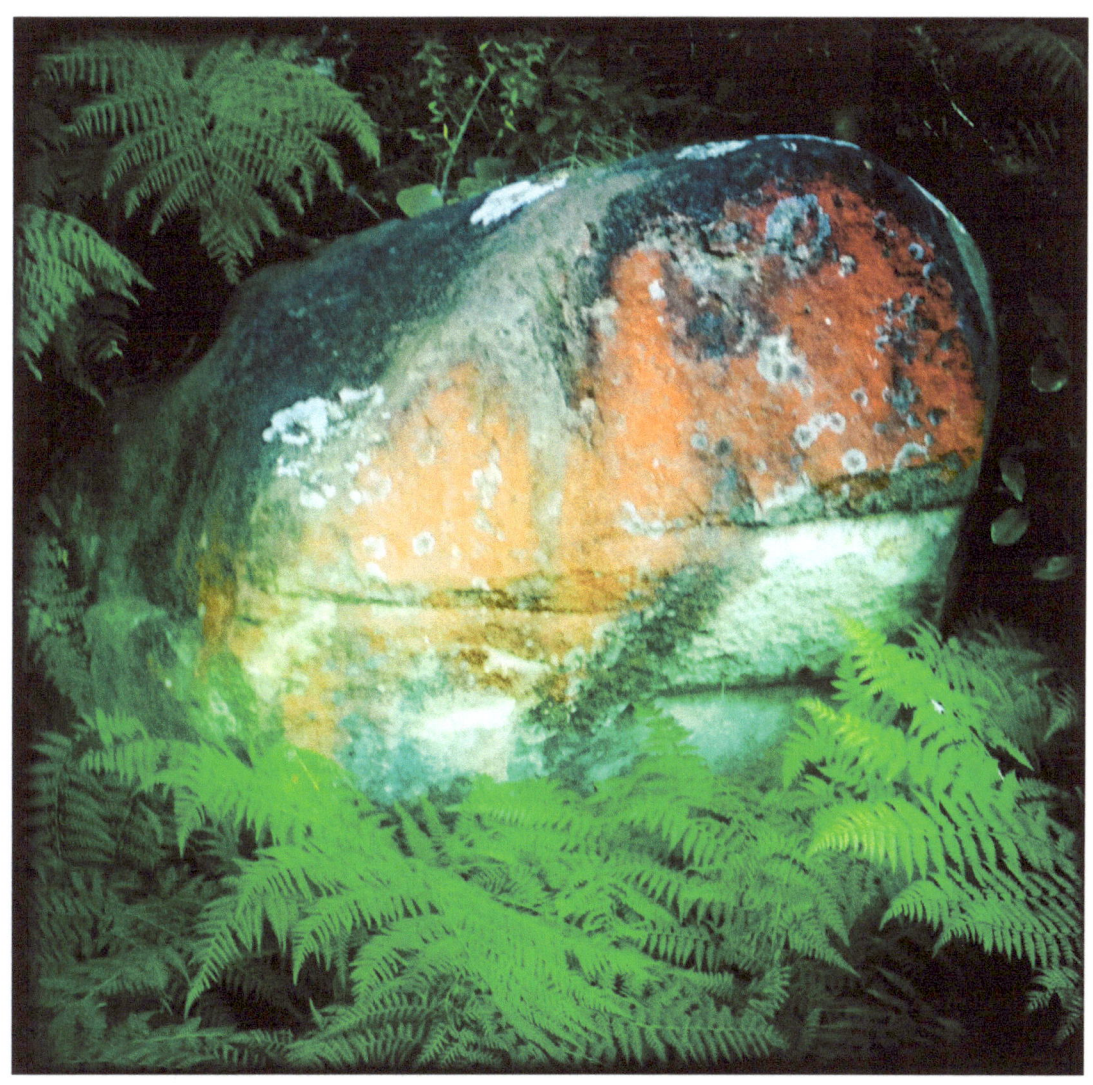

A friend of mine once read a 900 page white paper on what happens when you look at a photograph on a computer monitor.

I told him he wasted his time. It is not necessary to know all that detail, but it is necessary to:

- Use a monitor designed to display photographs properly, not a $199 monitor.
- View the monitor in the right lighting conditions.
- Make sure the monitor is adjusted properly.

Getting this right is a bit like tuning a musical instrument and then playing it where there is no background noise.

The process of doing this is called *Calibration*. No computer monitors are perfect out of the box, though some are close. Some monitors cannot ever be *calibrated* as they are too old or just brand new trash.

If you are obsessive compulsive about making sure what you see on your monitor looks like what is printed, you will have to come to terms with *calibration*.

Colour Management is a related process, which attempts to make every image look the same on screen, in print, in a book, or on a website.

Unfortunately making an image look the same everywhere is IMPOSSIBLE, but you have to try and get it as close as you can.

People who are good at this can reproduce a watercolour painting, for example, that looks just like the original. I have seen an artist fooled, by a reproduction, for a moment.

The photograph on the right shows I am trying hard by using a *calibration spyder* to read my computer monitor and adjust it to what it should be. This works most of the time.

Photographing it with my *iPhone* and the *Hipstamatic* app ensures the colour you see here is irrevocably wrong, even if it looks interesting.

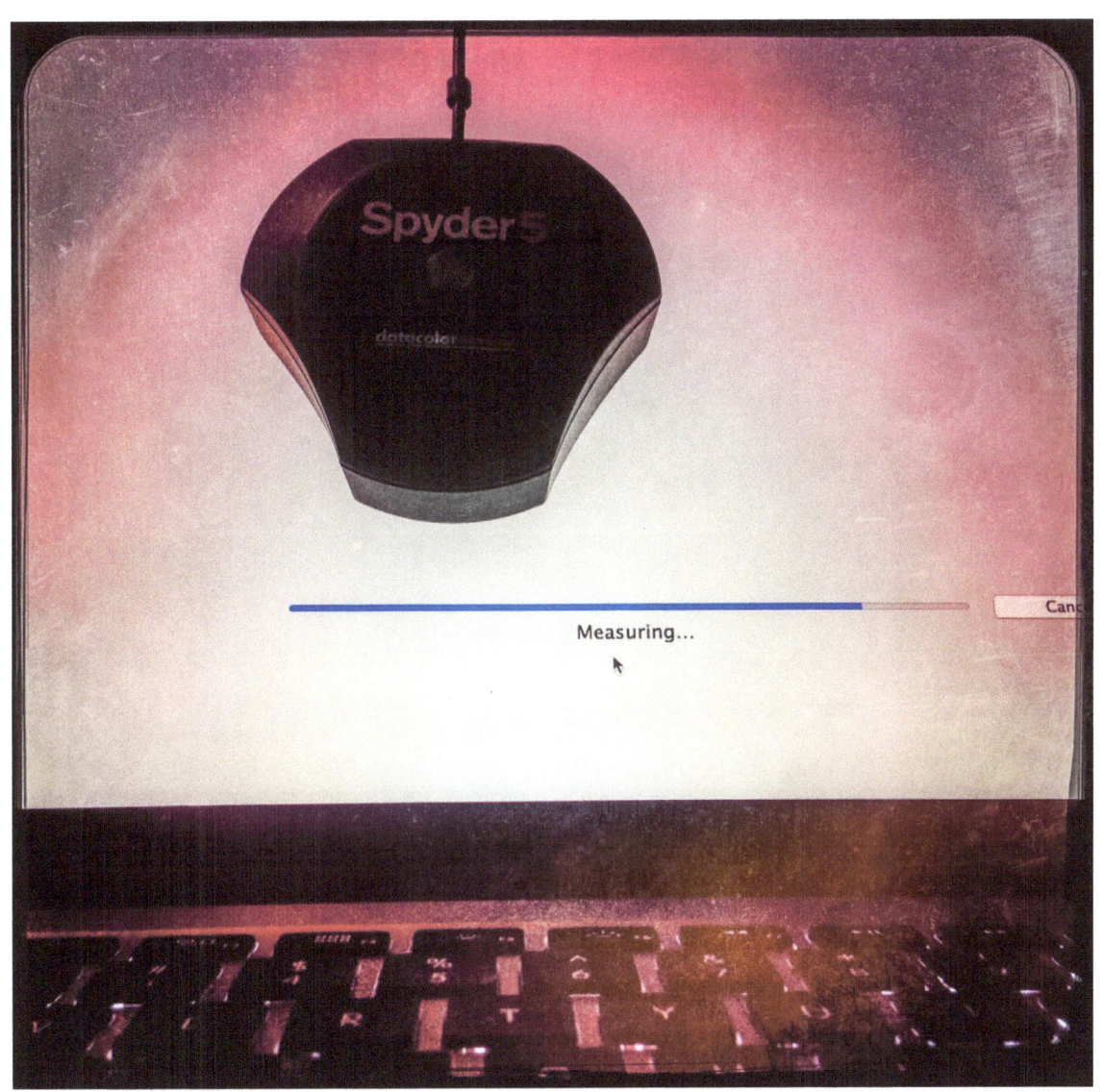

Taken by a moment of *patriotic fervour,* I photographed my shadow in salute, like a soldier going off to war. Later I found a man draping a flag over himself. Flags keep rain off too.

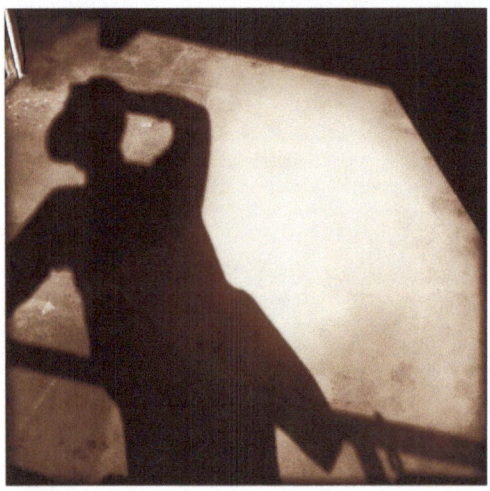

Red and blue are an archetypal colour combination that finds its way onto flags more than other colours, with consequent effects on world peace and harmony, or otherwise.

Our approach to flags and symbols as representations of nation, race and even football teams are interesting and at times troubling.

Artist *Joseph Beuys* was troubled not so much by flags, as by what they represent and what is done in their name.

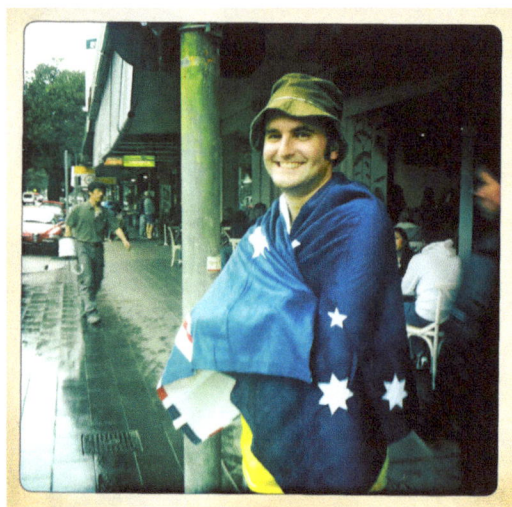

Serving with the German air force during WWII, he was the sole survivor of a plane crash and was quickly redeployed into action.

Before the war ended, he received a *Gold Wound Badge* for being injured in combat more than five times. The art he produced after the war had something to say but was never pretty.

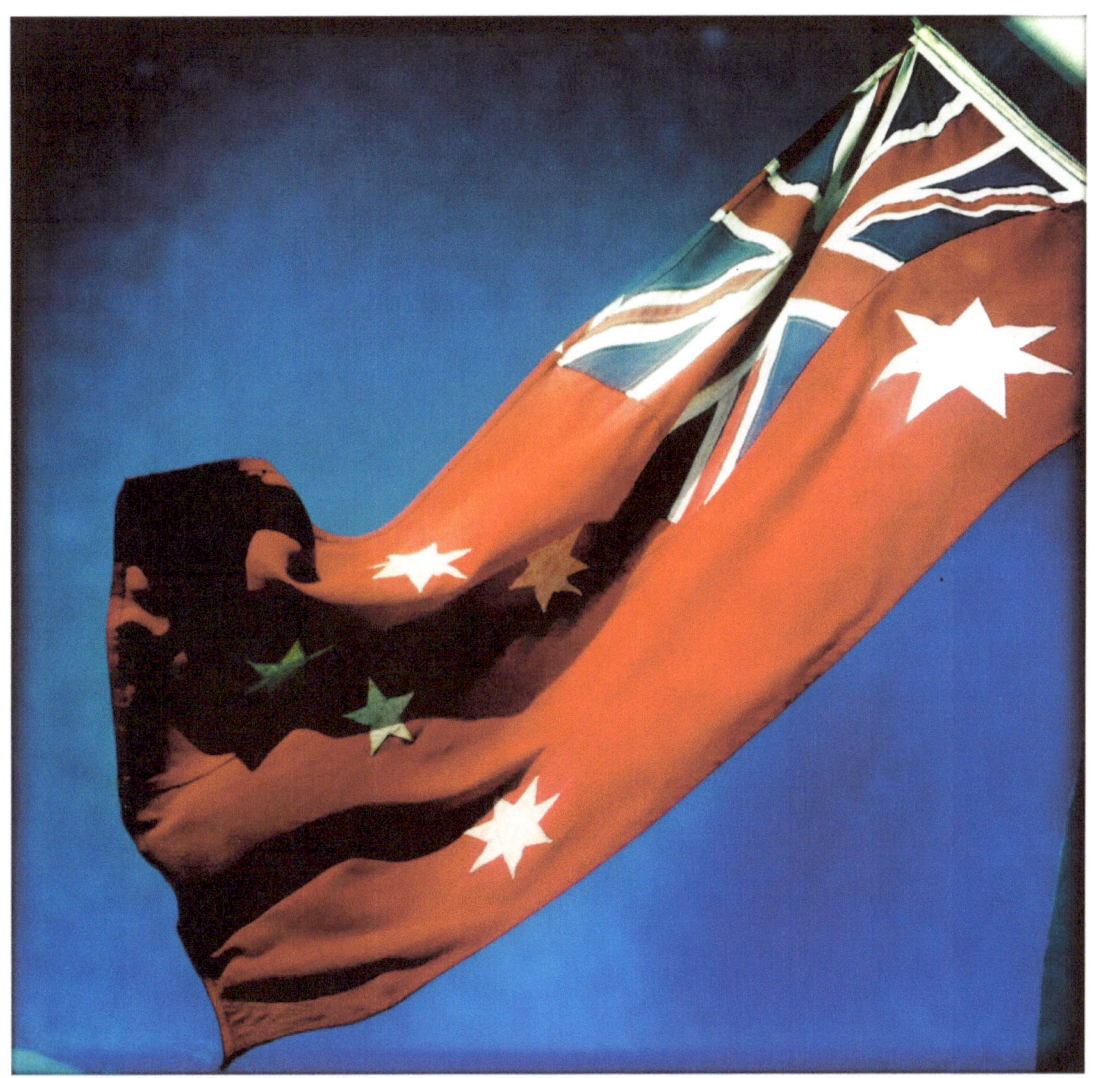

On this spread I am simply playing with colour. Overleaf, I have finally managed to get *Hipstamatic* to deliver a good blue & yellow image.

Blue & yellow is the most archetypal of the colour combinations and it always works. It does not take much yellow to stand against a lot of blue.

You might notice that despite living in a chaos rich world, I have a yearning for simplicity as evidenced by my periodic photographic reversions to the dictum of the *Bauhaus*.

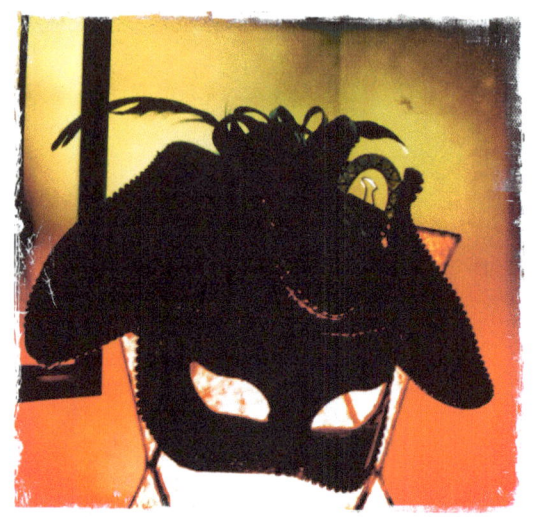

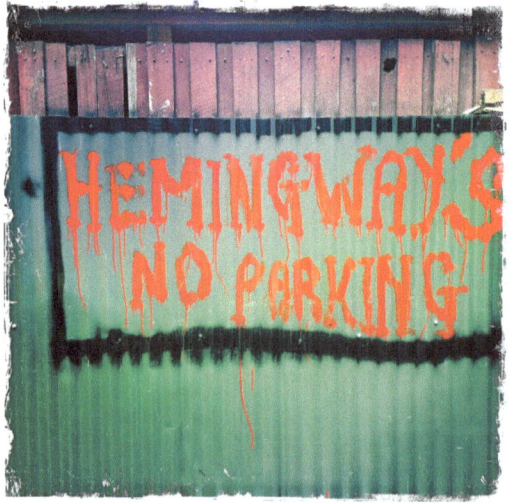

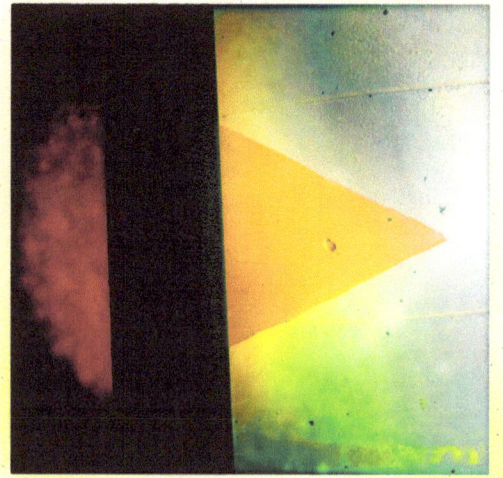

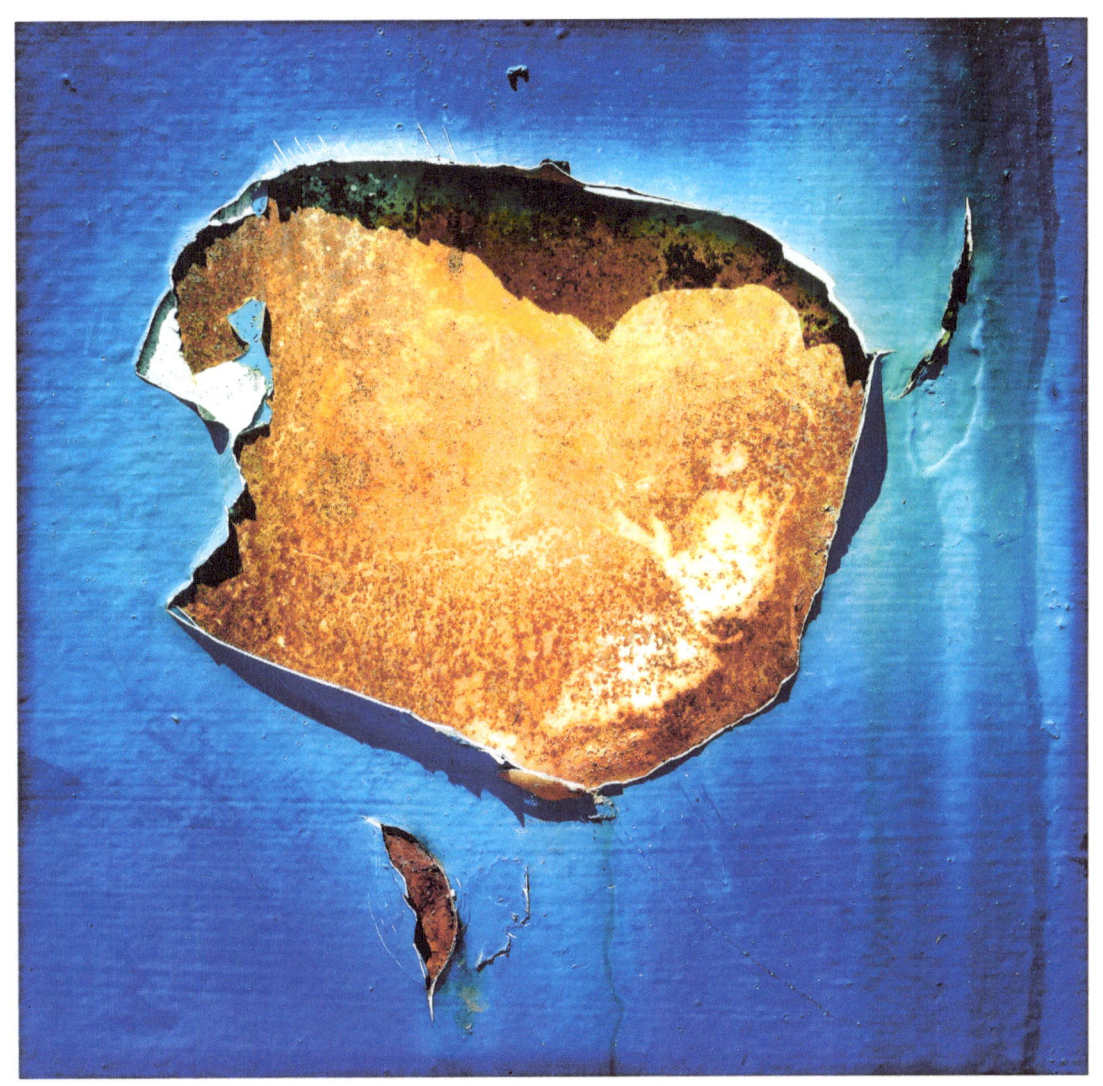

When I started with photography in a serious way, I did so with *colour transparency film* and reading the *Focal Guide to Photography* cover to cover, three times.

The beauty of *colour transparency film* (also known as *reversal film*) is standardised processing. What you photographed was what you got back from the lab, exactly.

Negative film is the opposite. What you photograph is **not** what you get. There is huge scope for interpretation between the negative and the print. *Ansel Adams* devoted an entire book to the art of untruthfully printing negatives to make better prints.

People used to think they were rotten photographers when a pimply lab operator printed negatives green and dark. Or felt like photographic maestros when a good lab operator endlessly fixed poor *exposure* and colour without ever letting them know.

iPhone photography is a bit like my original colour photography MINUS

the level of photographic control over the camera I am used to.

Strangely, it took the digital revolution for me to really understand and use *Black & White (B&W)*. Understanding *B&W* film theory from the *Focal Guide to Photography* and from *Ansel Adams* allowed me to quickly understand and use digital *B&W*.

I am finishing off this section with some gratuitously *over-saturated eye candy* for its own sake. Note how colour can often be used as a *compositional device*.

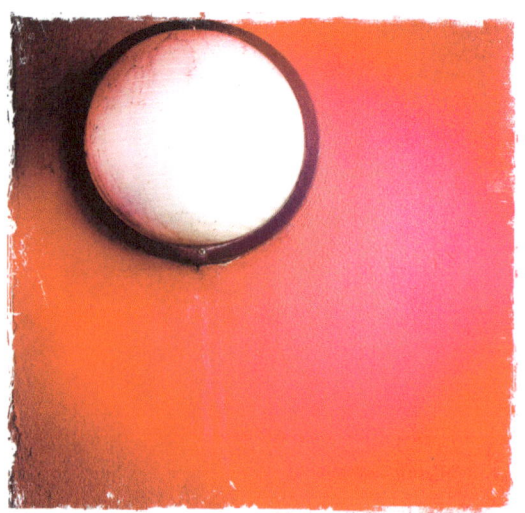

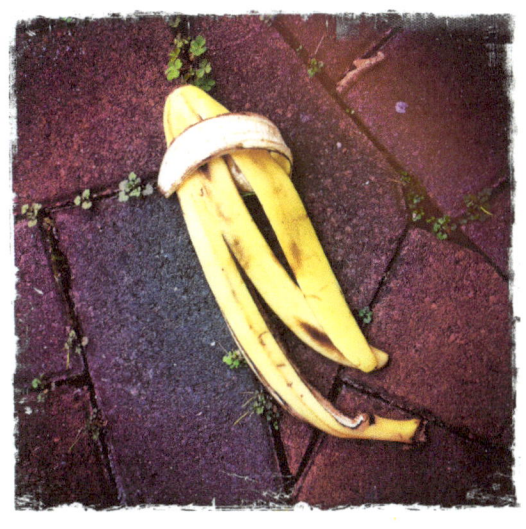

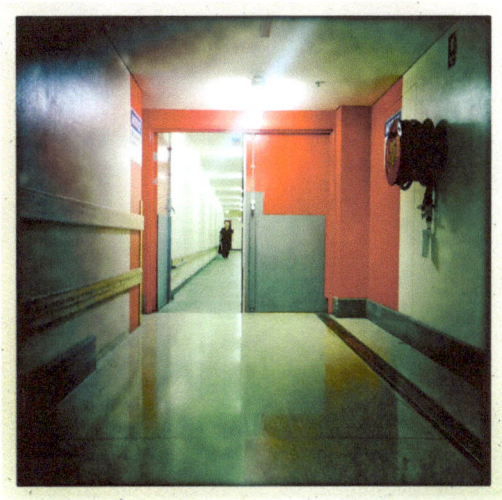

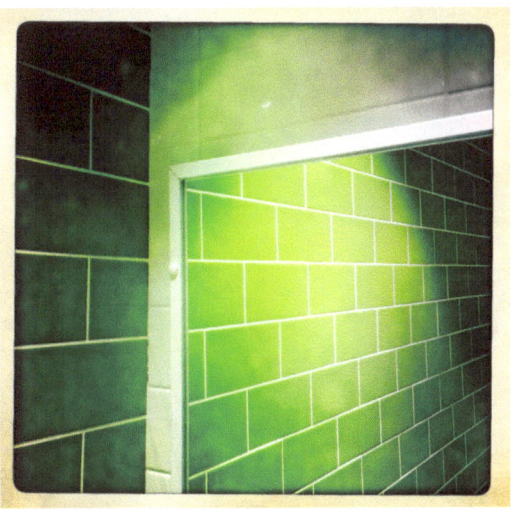

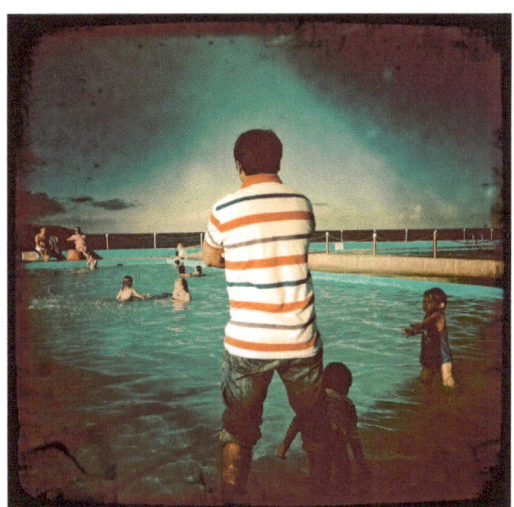

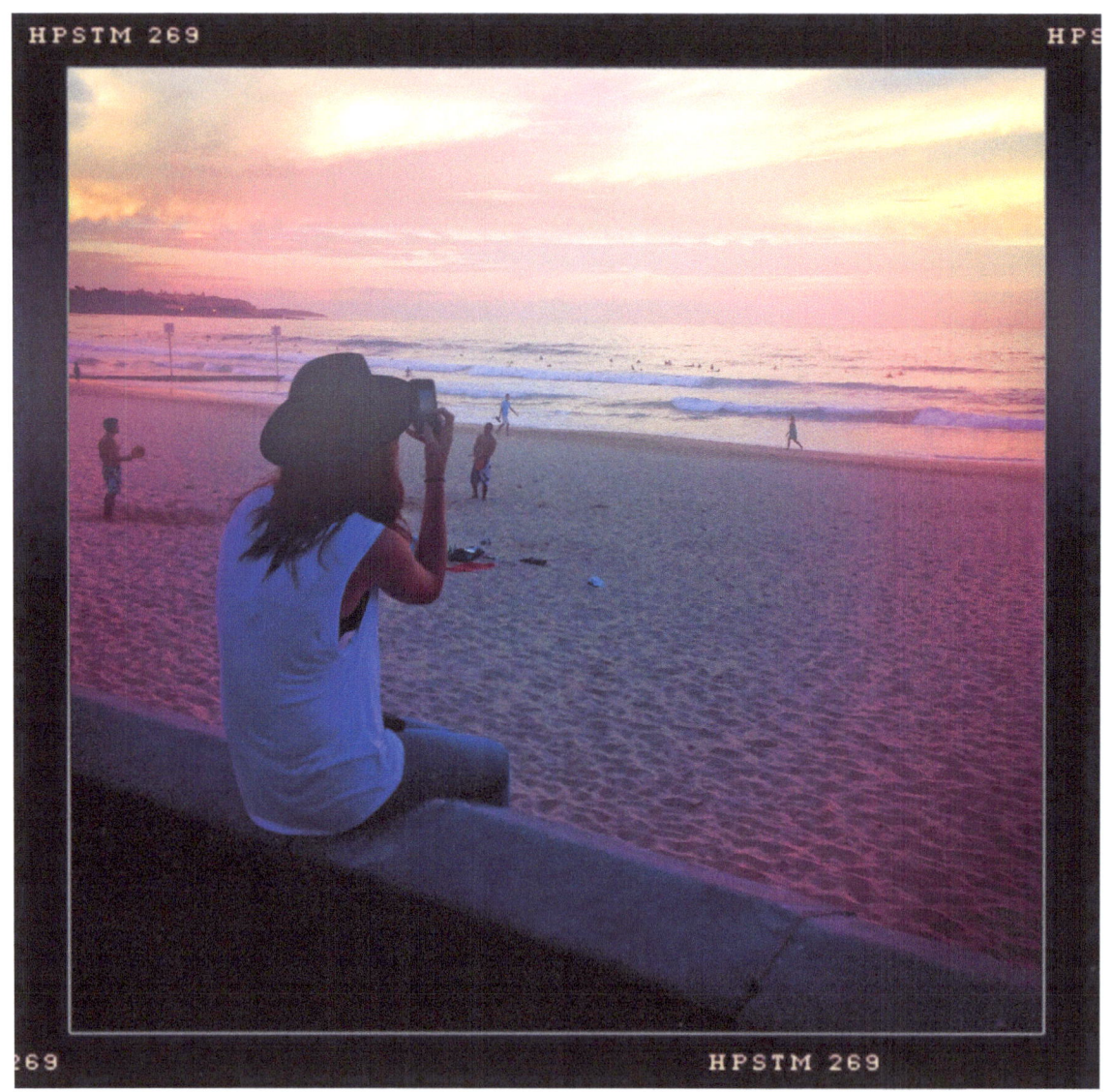

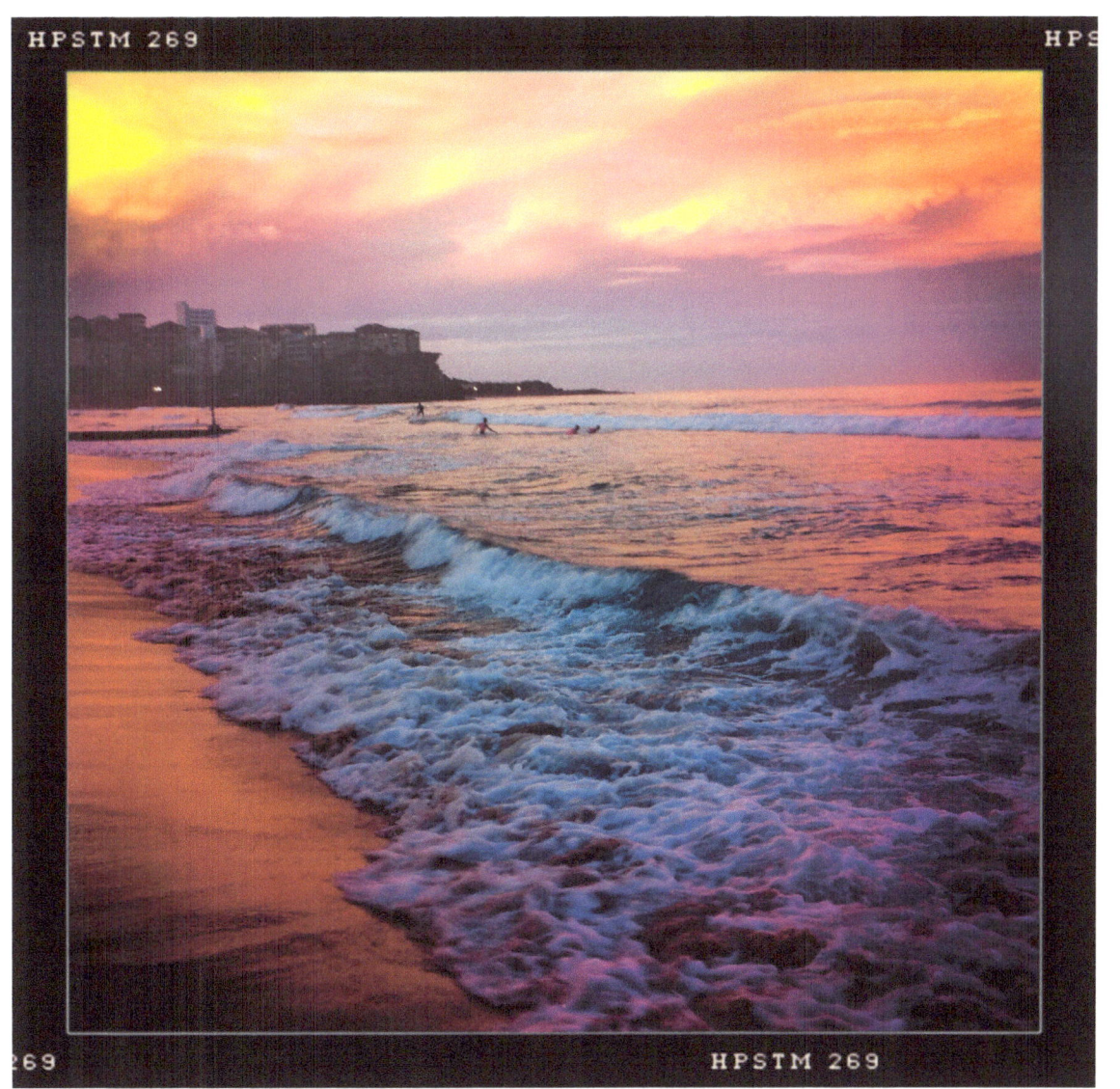

This man, image right, who is incidentally very good at kickboxing and selling smartphones, seems unaware of his shadow whilst communing with his smartphone, prior to spending a day selling smartphones.

I am making sure his shadow (of which he is unaware) is behaving itself and grab this image. The shadow completes the part of the story that is cropped out of the photograph.

This is an example of keeping photographic *composition* simple. The line of the concrete structure at the top is an important element as without it, the photograph becomes too empty and the shadow floats.

I converted the photo to *B&W*, as by this stage of this book and my life, I wanted to revisit the magic of *B&W*.

On the following spread I have again broken the layout rules of this book and included a pair of photographs on the same spread, rather than text left and photograph right, which is the classic recipe for photography books.

No text left and photo only right is even more classic, more absolutely totally purist, which I am not.

Really, I ran out of things to write and needed do some house cleaning, my accounts, iron the sheets - OR - put two photographs on one spread and keep working on this book.

Overleaf, sometimes shadows tell us everything we need to know:

It's a Tree!

Sometimes shadows in photographs mess with our minds (as they do if you are a novice to *Jungian Psychology* and the art of looking at your own shadow):

It's a small dog with big fluffy ears sitting in line with a shadow of the pole part of a small street sign. The dog's name is Dixie and her owner Vicki loves her dearly and pampers her lots. Lately Dixie has been pampered by Robert who has no competition for Dixie's attention when Vicki is at work.

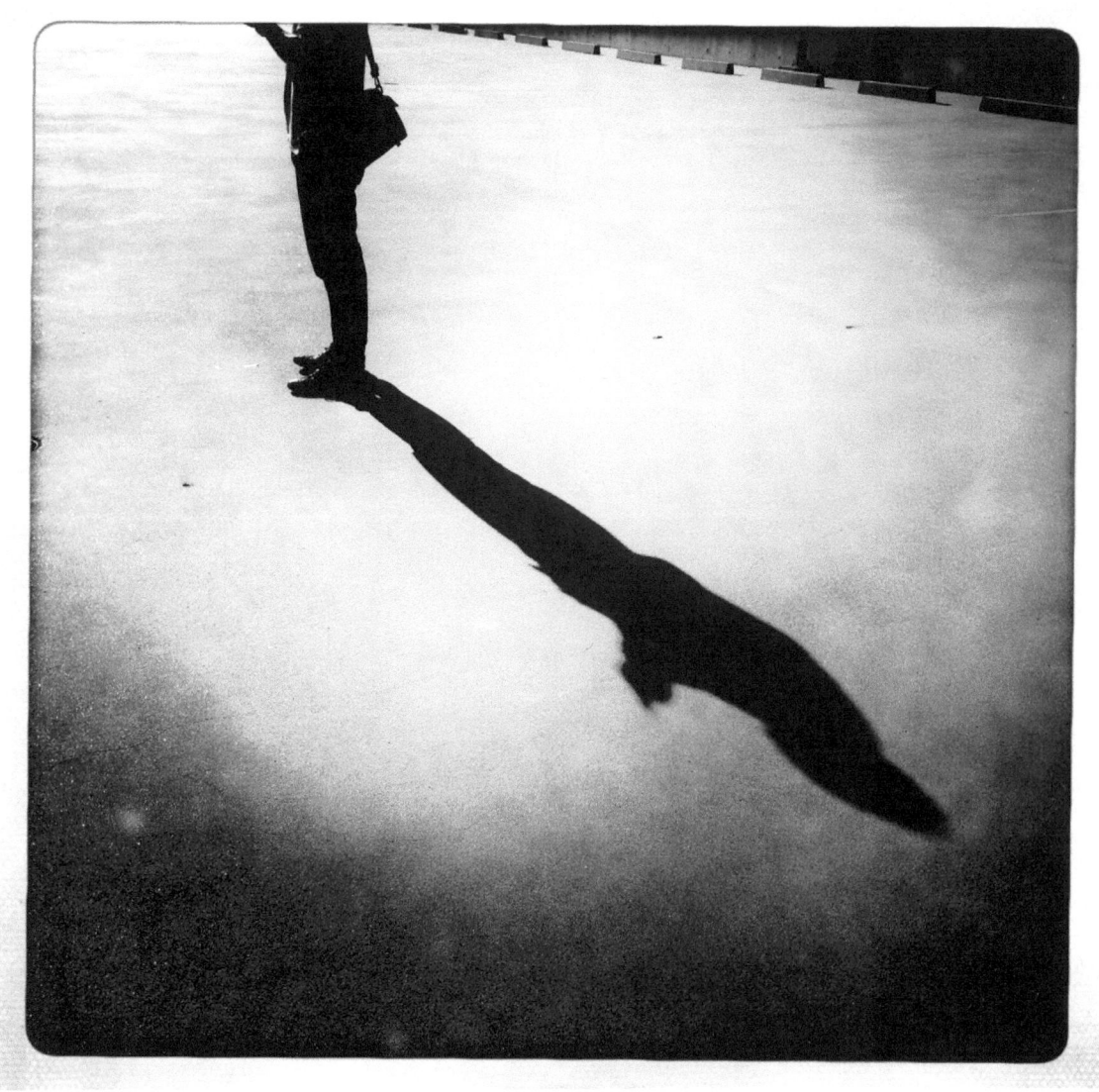

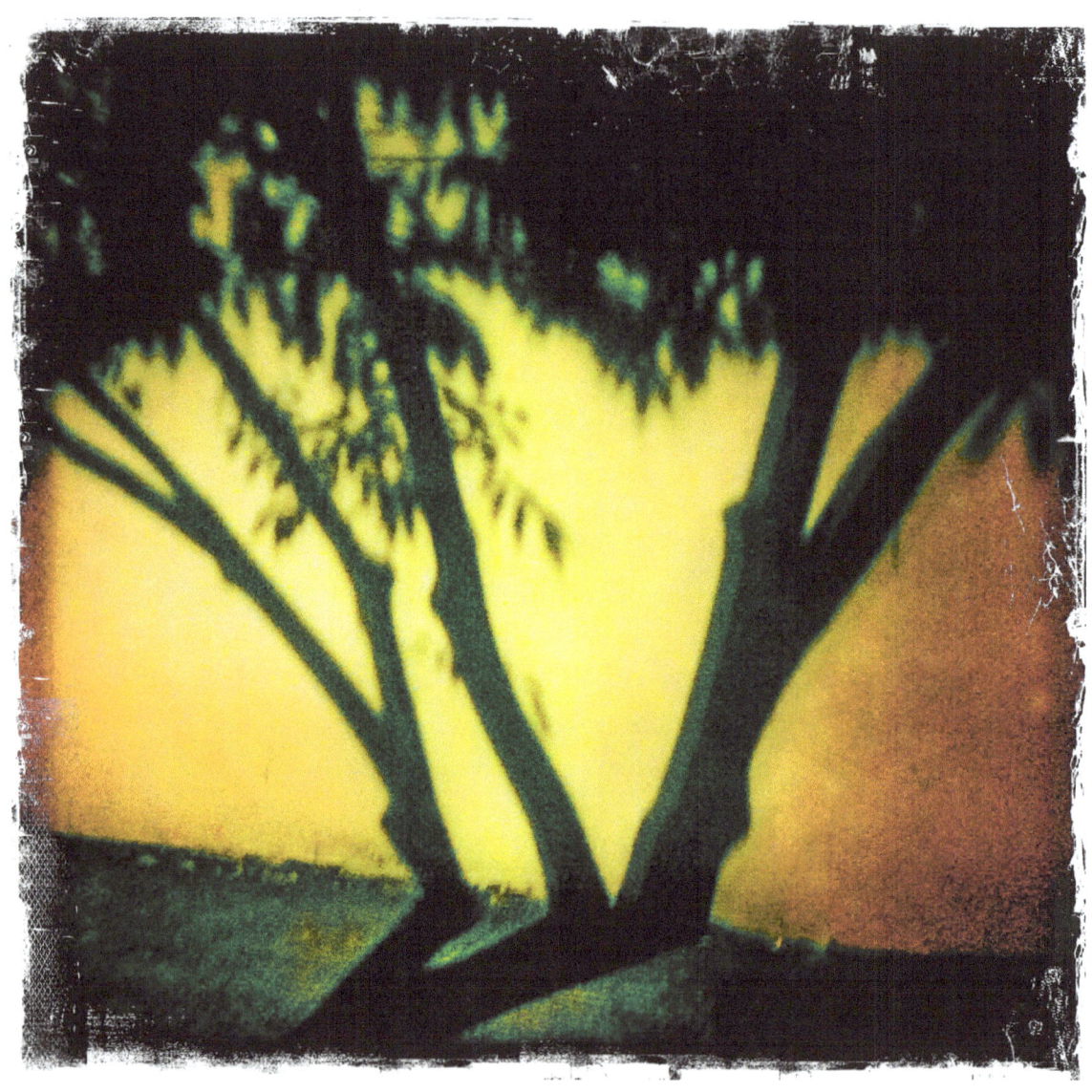

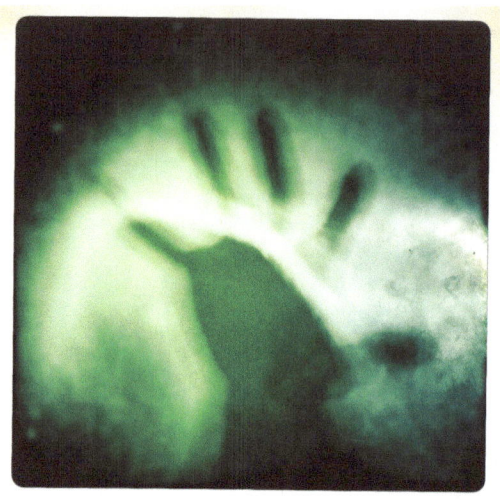

Shadows can be key or defining structural elements of photographs, rather than unwanted dark bits that get in the way of *correct exposure*.

The images on this page show how shadows can embellish or become the main elements of a visual story.

My favourite, overleaf, is of an earthworm that died on the steps of the National Gallery of Australia. Next to it was a V shaped twig. I added the *shadow play*. Even earthworms can *die in the name of art*.

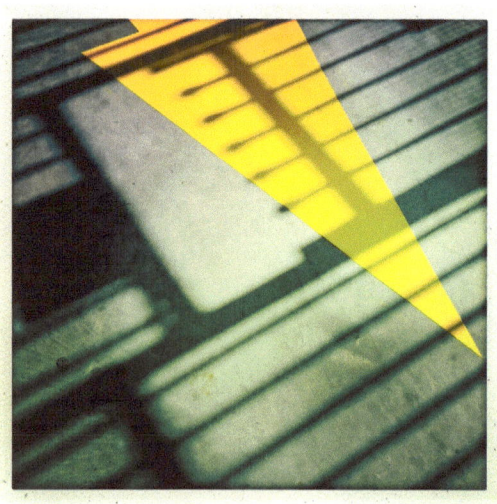

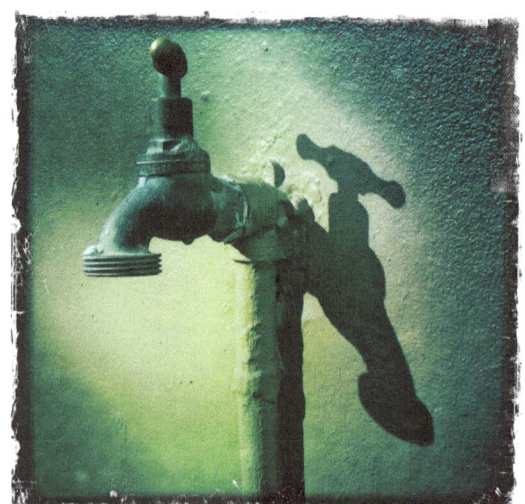

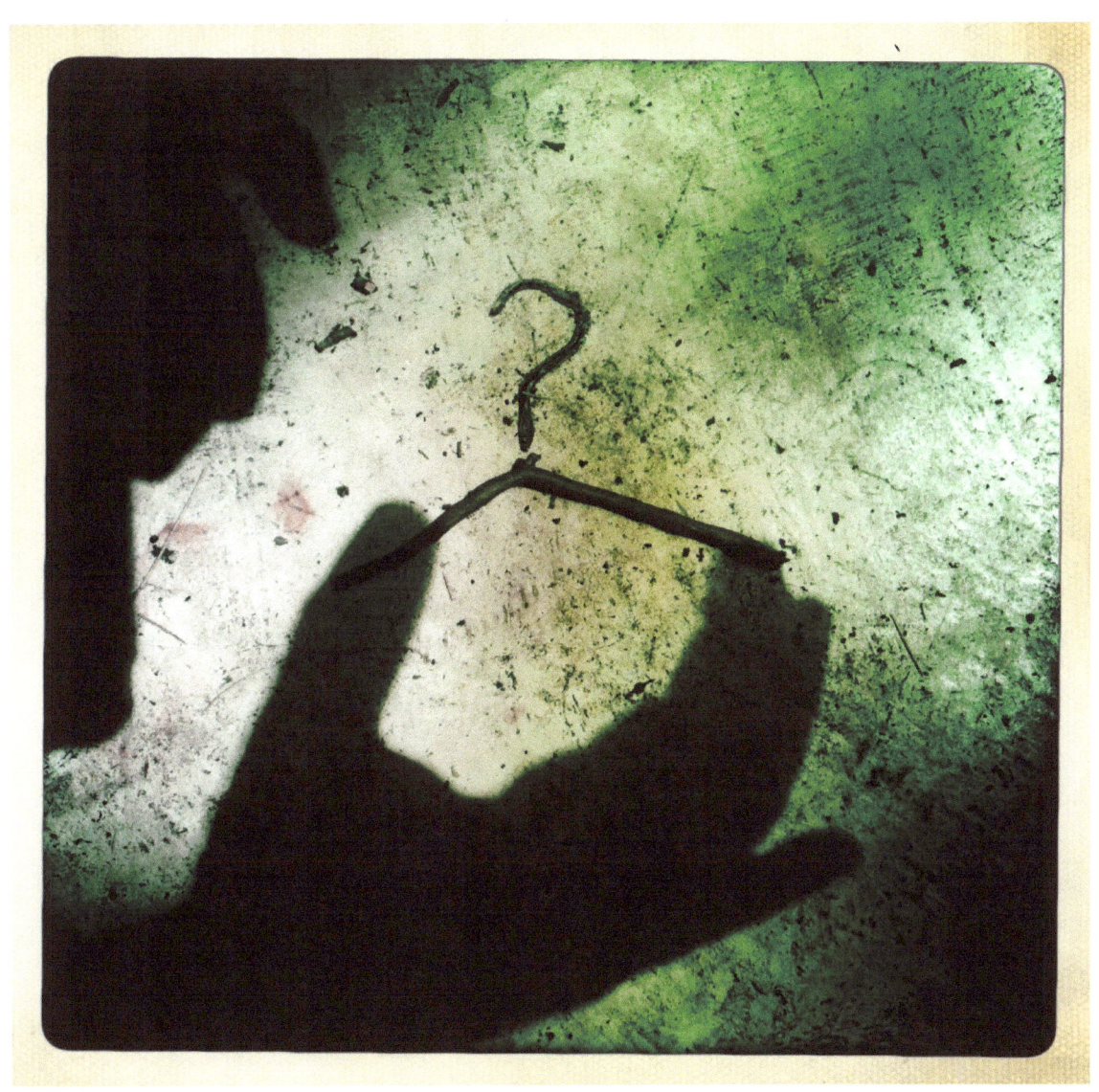

11

Selfies

Selfies, or *Self Portraits*, predate photography by over 3000 years. Some cultures don't do *selfies*. Some don't do portraits at all, or at least didn't until they got smartphones.

Right is a *selfie* that was approved for public release by my in-house PR Department, the one that lives in my head. Sometimes it has lapses and my carefully crafted public image takes a dive.

Even *selfies* of my shadow don't escape the watchful eye of my PR Department.

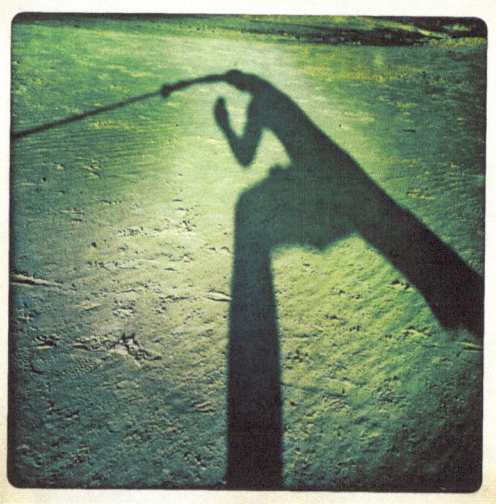

My in-house *spin doctor* and stylist get involved too.

The most notable contemporary *selfie* photographer was *Cindy Sherman*. She defined the category of dress-up *self-portraits*. They were carefully stage-managed in every respect, nothing was left to accident.

She dressed up and role played every female stereotype she could think of and it kept her going for years and years.

Sometimes *selfies* are genuine portraits, but more commonly, one's PR Department becomes involved and the real story lives off picture.

Have you noticed the in-focus bananas behind me? Photography has an infuriating and fascinating ability to include and feature things we miss. How could this have gone into print?

After this, I am wondering who hired my in-house PR manager and how is it my retouch artist still has a job?

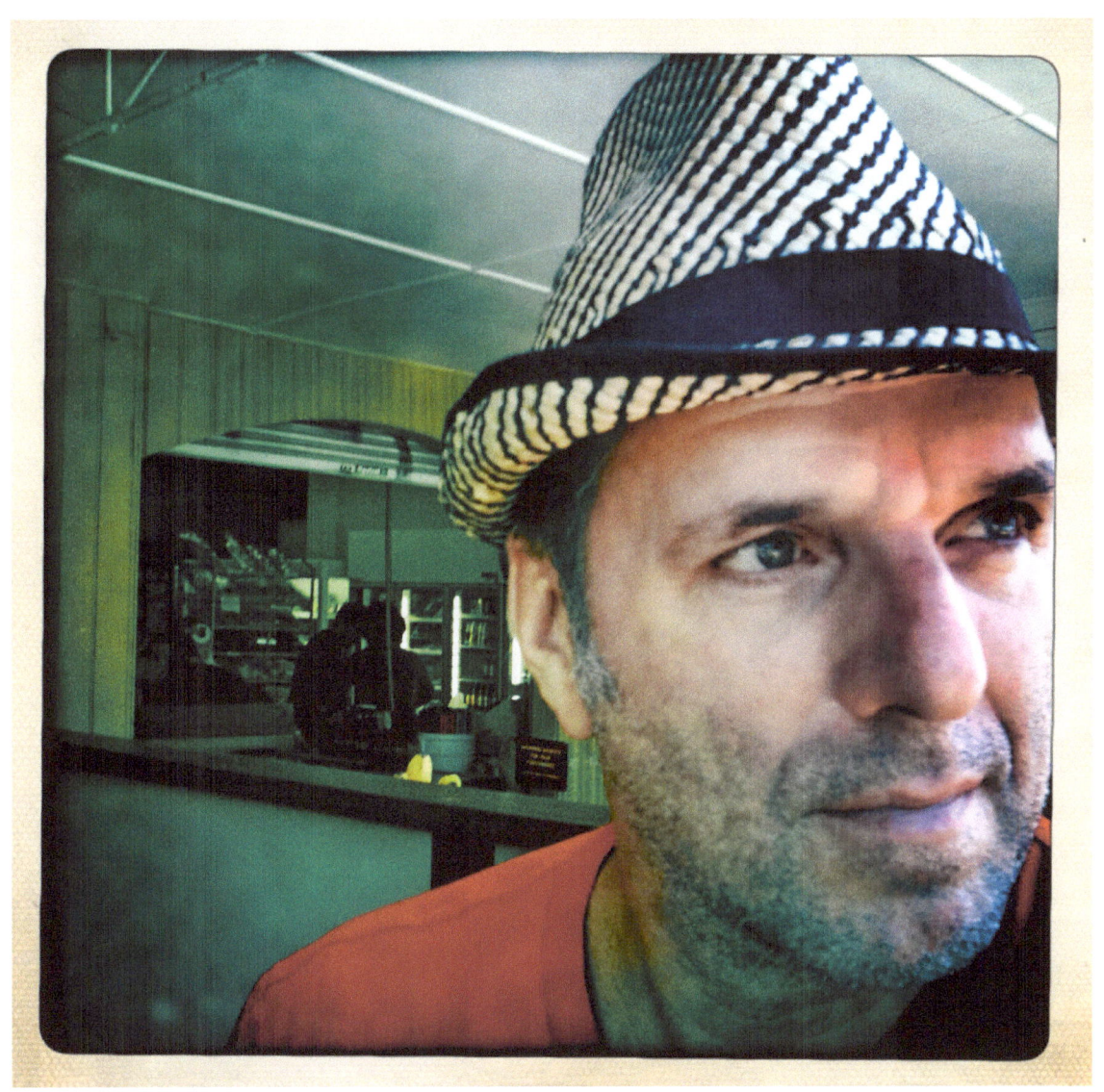

12

The Inside of my Pocket

This could never happen with a *large format film camera*, or even a *digital SLR camera*. But the *iPhone* manages to photograph the inside of my pocket, a photographic space hitherto less documented than the *dark side of the Moon*.

The dark image opposite looks like a film trick I used to do that exploited the effects of *diffraction*. I think it's out of focus bits of light coming through the fabric of my pants.

Diffraction is best known for limiting the sharpness of any camera according to the *f number* of the lens and the size of the pixel sites on the sensor. The smaller the physical pixels on the camera sensor and the larger the *f number,* the more *diffraction* blurs the image.

When a photographic system is *diffraction limited, diffraction* rather than optical design or any other factor, limits sharpness. It's one of those laws of the universe things that can't be beaten by technology.

Photographers of the *f64 Group* did not care about photographing the insides of their pockets or about *diffraction* as they used *cameras* with film sizes from 5x4 inches to 11x14 inches. These are the sizes of the sheets of film they put inside their cameras, not the prints they made.

With 8x10 inch (203x254 mm) film for example, *diffraction* is nowhere the issue it is with a 1/3" (3.6x4.8 mm) *iPhone* 5s to 7 camera sensor.

These *iPhone* cameras with an f2.2 or f1.8 lens and 8-12 MP, are on the verge of being *diffraction limited*.

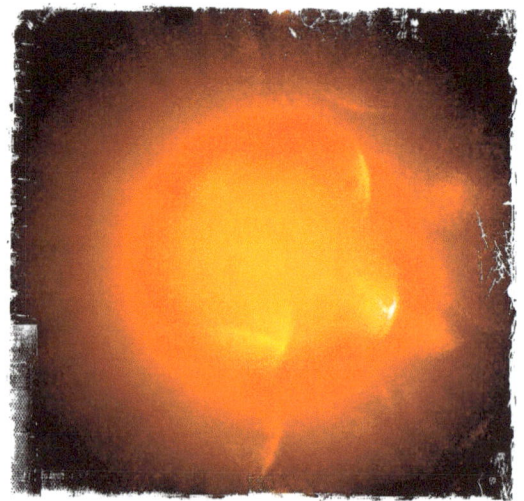

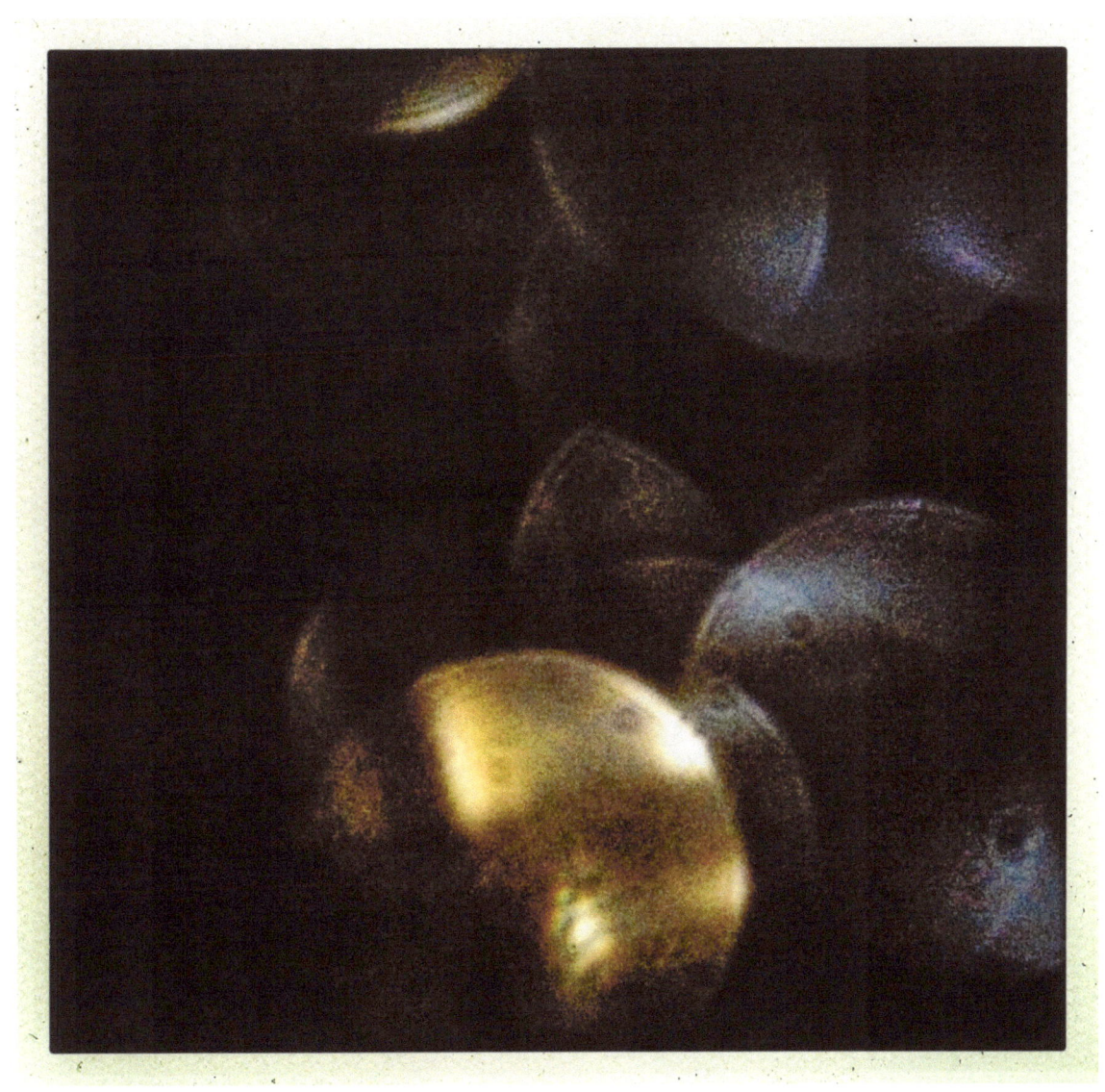

If one put a 40MP sensor of the same size behind the same lens, there would be no more detail, just 40 million *diffraction* caused blurry pixels.

The aperture of the *iPhone* lens does not change from its maximum, partially to simplify construction and partially to prevent loss of sharpness that would happen if it could be adjusted to smaller *aperture* sizes (bigger numbers) as happens with most cameras.

I can't help myself, this section was meant to be light fun.

So, out of my pocket with the *iPhone*. The image at traffic lights in the rain (overleaf), renders droplets less than one inch from the lens out of focus, but sharp focus in the distance. The out of focus droplets become circles and shapes that look a bit like the photos from inside my pocket.

IPhones (and small sensor cameras) have a very large *depth of field* (what's in focus) due to the very short *focal length* of their lenses: 4.12 mm for the *iPhone* 6.

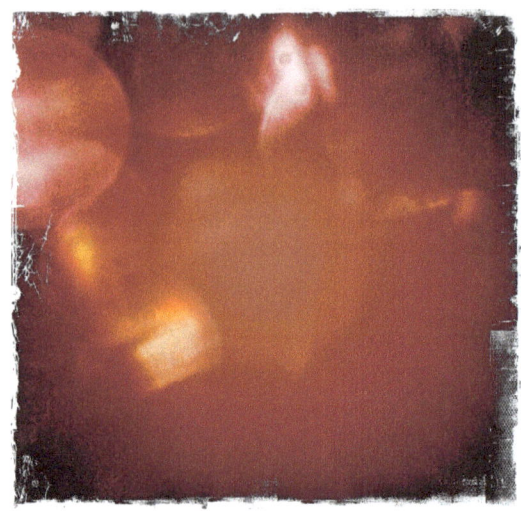

We fixate on *megapixels*, but real visual detail, *dynamic range*, *colour depth* and *signal to noise ratio* are also vital for good images. Simplistic marketing avoids this multi-dimensional complexity.

The size of pixel sites in the sensor is crucial as this determines how much light each gathers. The small *iPhone* sensor gathers less than 2% as much light as a 24x36 mm DSLR camera sensor and loses much as a result. That however is also the source of its charm.

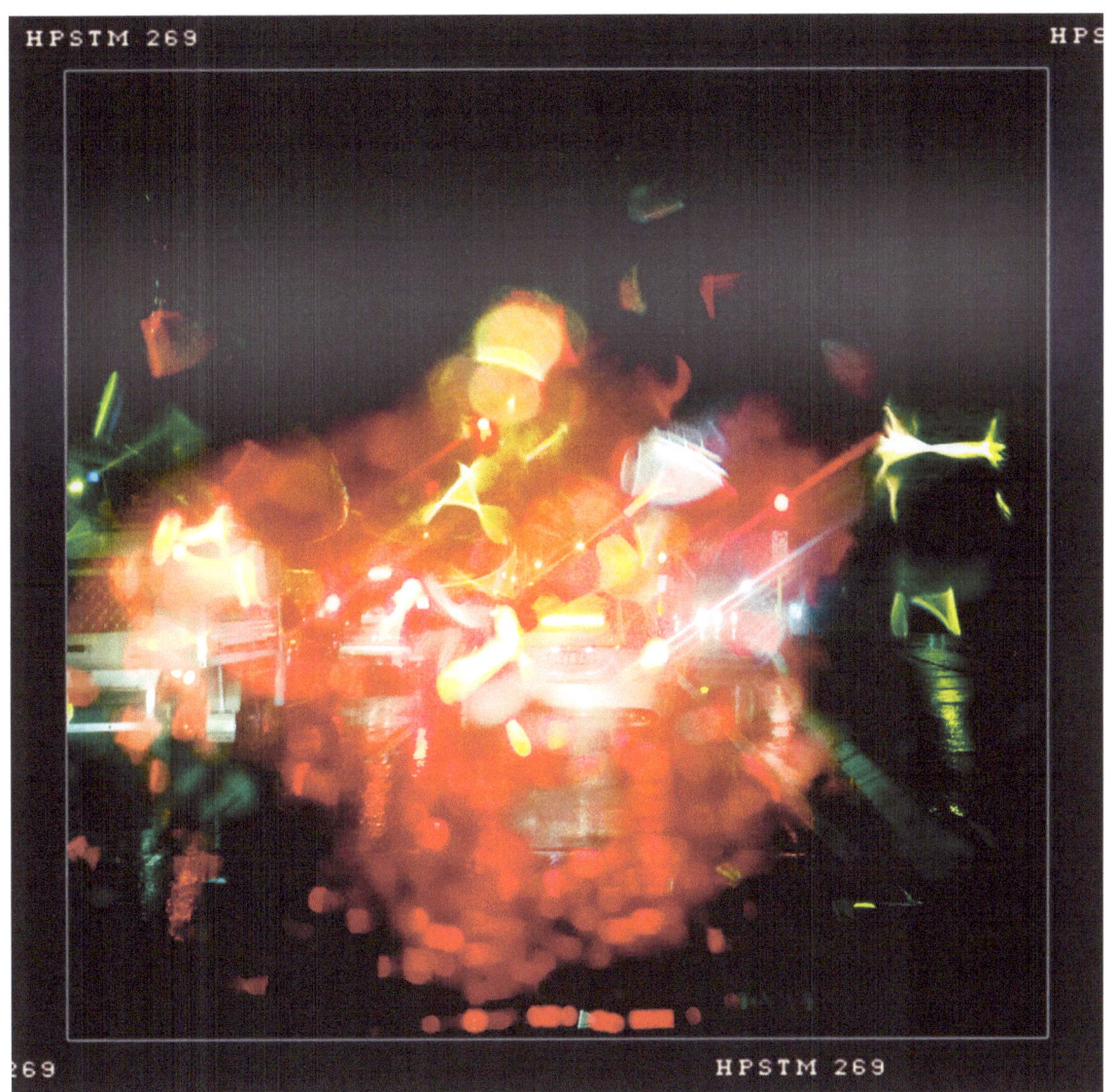

13

Photographing what is NOT there

The cat's chair. Photographing things or people that are missing, or even painting them, is nothing new. *Van Gogh* painted *Gauguin's Chair* without *Gauguin*.

Gauguin left France for Tahiti with his painting kit and modern art, if not *Gauguin* himself, was better for that.

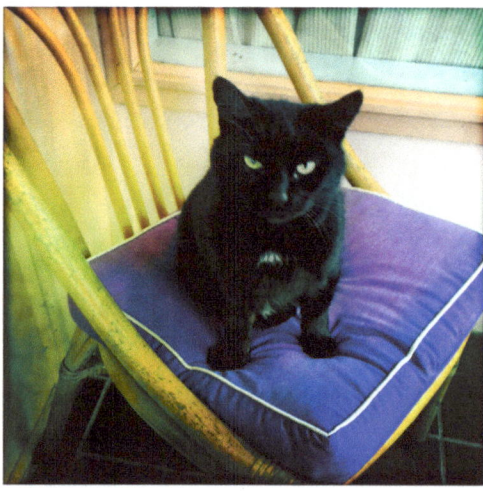

The reason the cat's chair is empty is the poor cat died. I photographed its empty cat chair knowing at least the *Van Gogh* part of the history of creating images of chairs with the occupant missing.

During the *Crimean War*, *Roger Fenton* took a photograph of a field littered with cannon balls, no corpses in sight, and entitled it "*The Valley of the Shadow of Death*". *Fenton* did not photograph corpses. In this case it is their absence from his photograph that screams.

We are all walking talking libraries of images we have seen before and these WILL come out in what you photograph (or draw or paint).

You can become a more effective photographer by studying what has happened before. This point in image history is the leading edge of an evolution of imagery that started with cave painting. Clever photography is knowingly merging what has happened before with what is happening now and of course, adding your own spin.

If you don't study history you will think that pointing a camera up or at an angle is a new idea, when the reality is that *Rodchenko* was doing that when (or even before) your grandparents were in nappies.

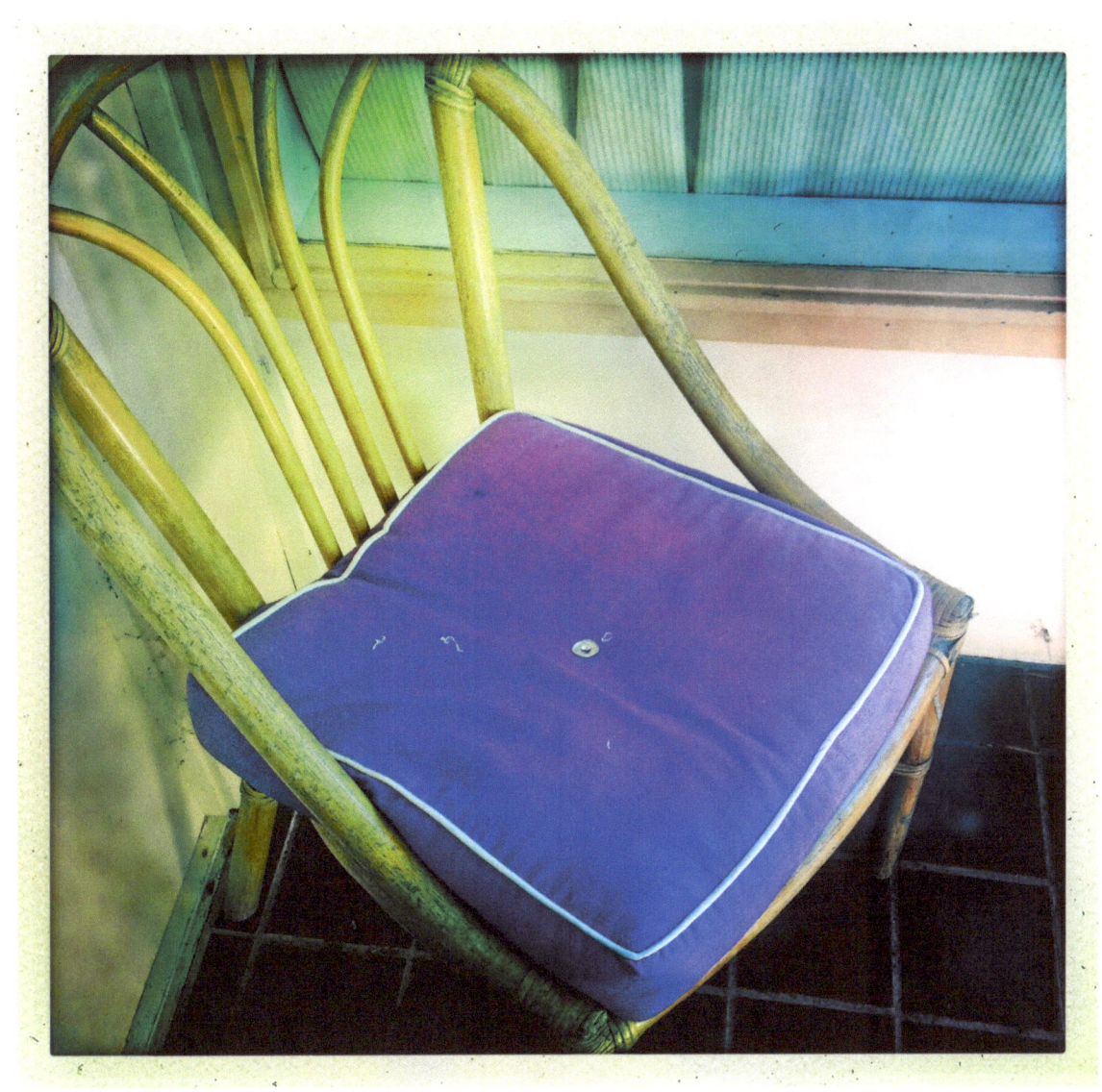

Not only has this dog been lost, but its memory has been cruelly banished by destruction of its photograph.

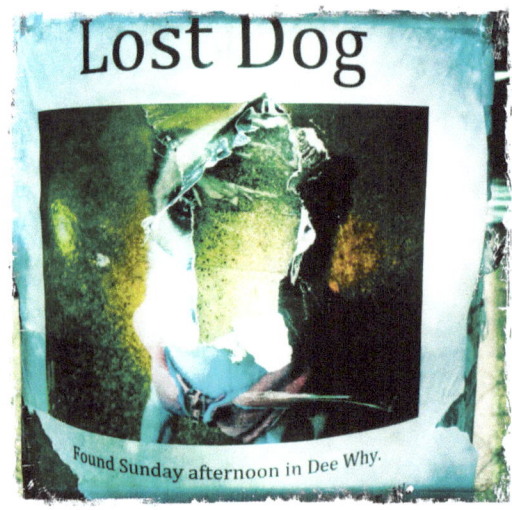

Lost Dog

Found Sunday afternoon in Dee Why.

Photography has a remarkable ability to lock in "truths", memories and emotions. One social media platform now shows me old photos I have posted, reminding me it holds my memories, a scary prospect.

When we, or our political nations change, memories often need to be altered, rewritten or removed. A friend once *Photoshopped* another woman over a photograph of his ex-wife on a gondola in Venice.

David Hockney referred to this as *Stalanist Photography*, after *Stalin's* propensity to murder countless people repugnant to his politics, and then after the event, to alter the photographic record accordingly.

A pair of photographs survive, both show a group of people, the earlier one with *Stalin* and *Trotsky* side by side. But in the later photo there is NO *Trotsky*. *Trotsky* was assassinated in Mexico. Most of his family were assassinated also.

Back in *Stalinist Russia*, our creative star *Rodchenko* roughly applied black ink to erase the faces and names of once favoured, now dead *Apparatchiks* featured in his ground-breaking, innovatively designed books and magazines. It appears he did this to prevent his own erasure.

Luckily, not everything that is not there is sinister or speaks of loss. Rose petals (not cannon balls) litter a field and tell us that a wedding has just been. I wish many happy years for the couple.

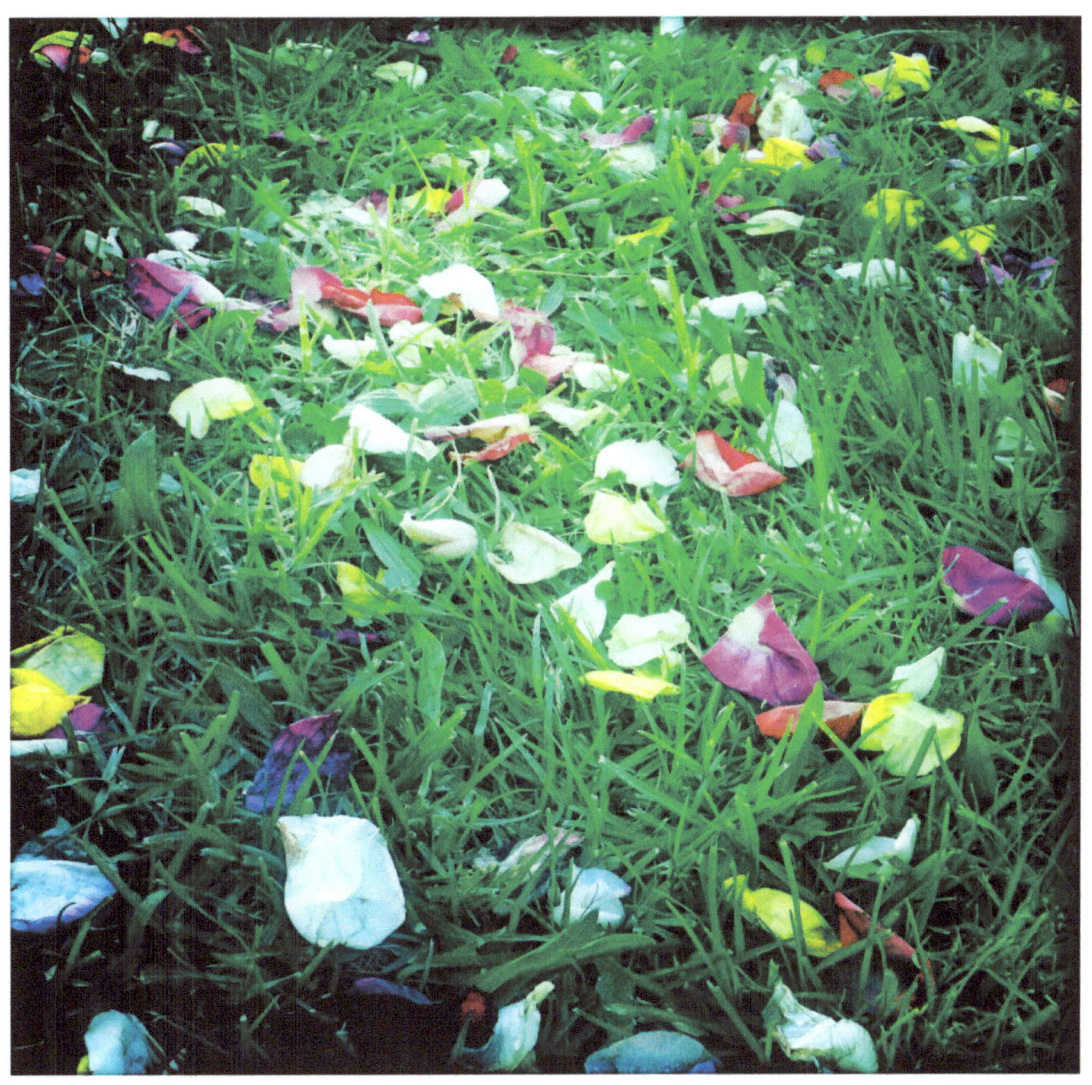

14

Rolling Shutter

Most small cameras and smart-phones do not have the *shutter mechanism* that larger cameras have. The click you hear is from the camera's speaker and serves only to reassure the photographer.

These *shutters* are *electronic*. When taking a photograph, the image sensor works like a flatbed scanner, assembling the image line by line, just a lot faster. This is called *Rolling Shutter*.

Rolling Shutter has no visible effect until the subject or the camera moves quickly. Then the image will become skewed one way or another. With a bit of trial and error you can work out which way the *shutter* scans and orient your camera or phone to get the direction of skew you want.

The *Rolling Shutter* effect is like the effect of a *Focal Plane Shutter* (a real mechanism) when it is used at *shutter speeds* above the *flash synchronisation* speed.

The *Focal Plane Shutter* dates back to 1883 and is now used in nearly all SLR and interchangeable lens cameras.

Another type of shutter is the *Leaf Shutter* which works radially and has no *rolling shutter* effect. It is located inside the lens next to the lens *aperture mechanism*.

The most used image to demonstrate the skewing effect of a *focal plane shutter* is of a racing car at the French Grand Prix, taken by *Jacques Henri Lartigue* in 1912. My attempt, right, is not as evocative as his original.

This skewing effect on modern cameras is less than in *Lartigue's* day as shutter mechanisms and film or sensor *sensitivity* are much higher, giving much shorter *exposure* times. Things have to move much faster for the skewing effect to appear.

For me, the wildest of *Lartigue's* photographs is of the remarkable *Bichonnade Leaping*, down a flight of stairs in the abundant attire of the day. Check out this photo and please do not ask anyone to jump like this...

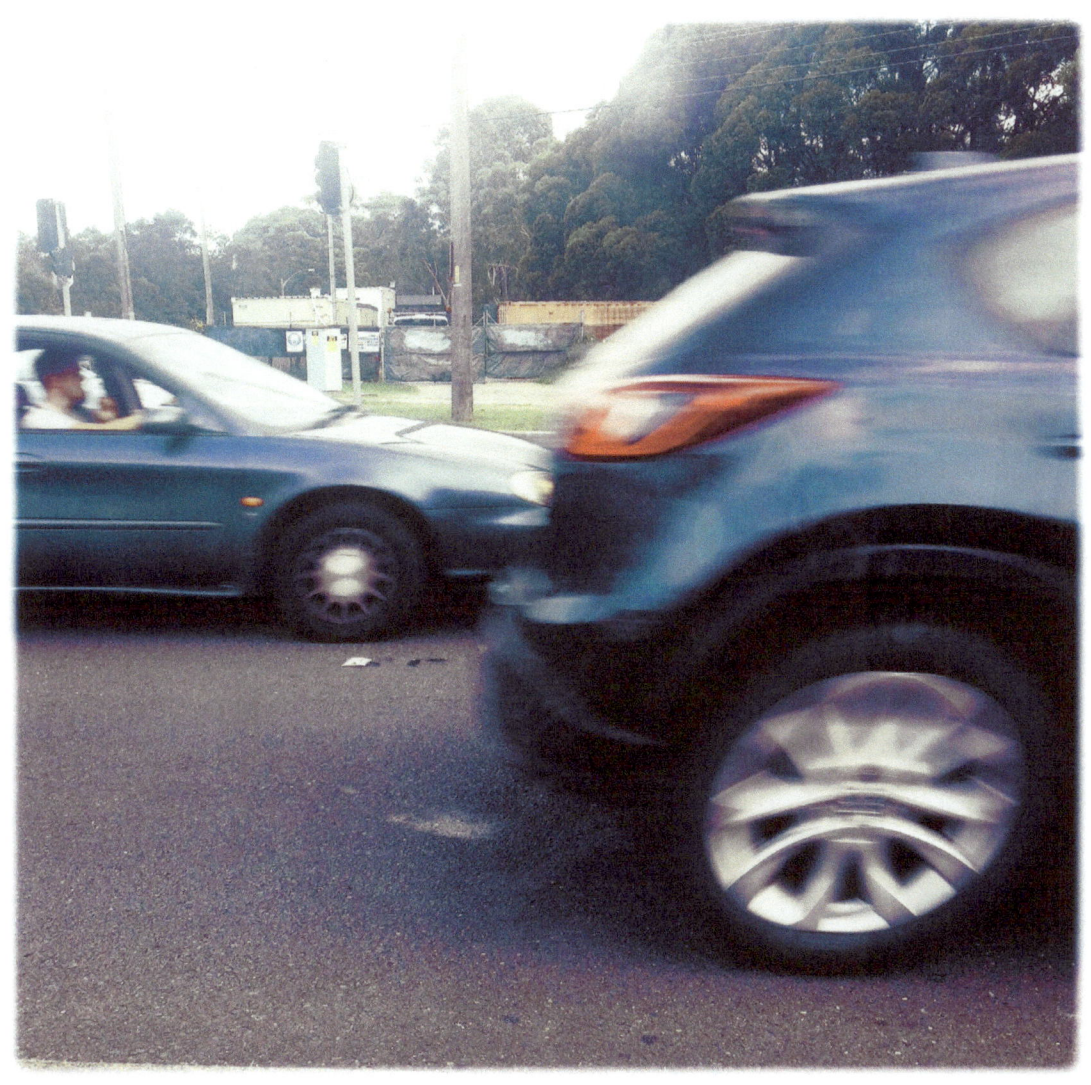

Another *Rolling Shutter* effect shows as banding in the image when photographing under electric *AC (Alternating Current)* lights. Lights powered by (*DC Direct Current*) do not flicker.

Alternating current reverses itself 50 times per second, with a short dark period between the reversals. Hence the banding when a *Rolling Shutter* camera is used. Some cameras detect and digitally try to reduce the *AC* flickering or banding effect.

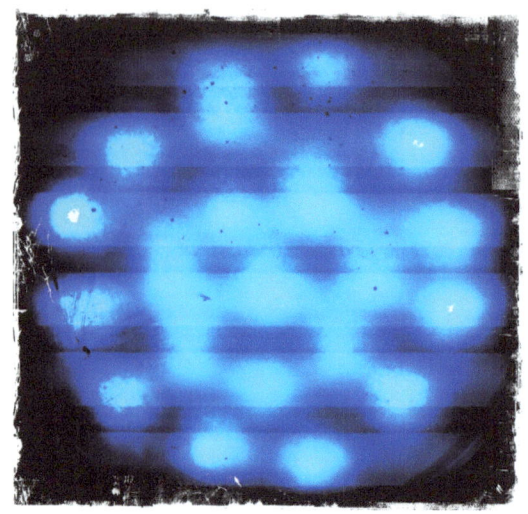

The large photo right is a circular light not a striped planet with dead insects on its equator.

We of course do not notice this *AC* oscillation as it is too quick for us to see. As in movies, we do not see the gaps between the rapidly changing stills of each movie frame.

The image above is a collection of LED lights flickering to the invisible *AC* rhythm. And below, rapidly moving water is compressed as the sensor is scanning against its flow.

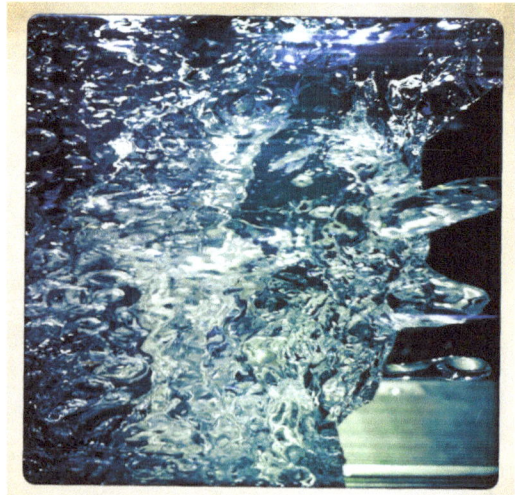

74

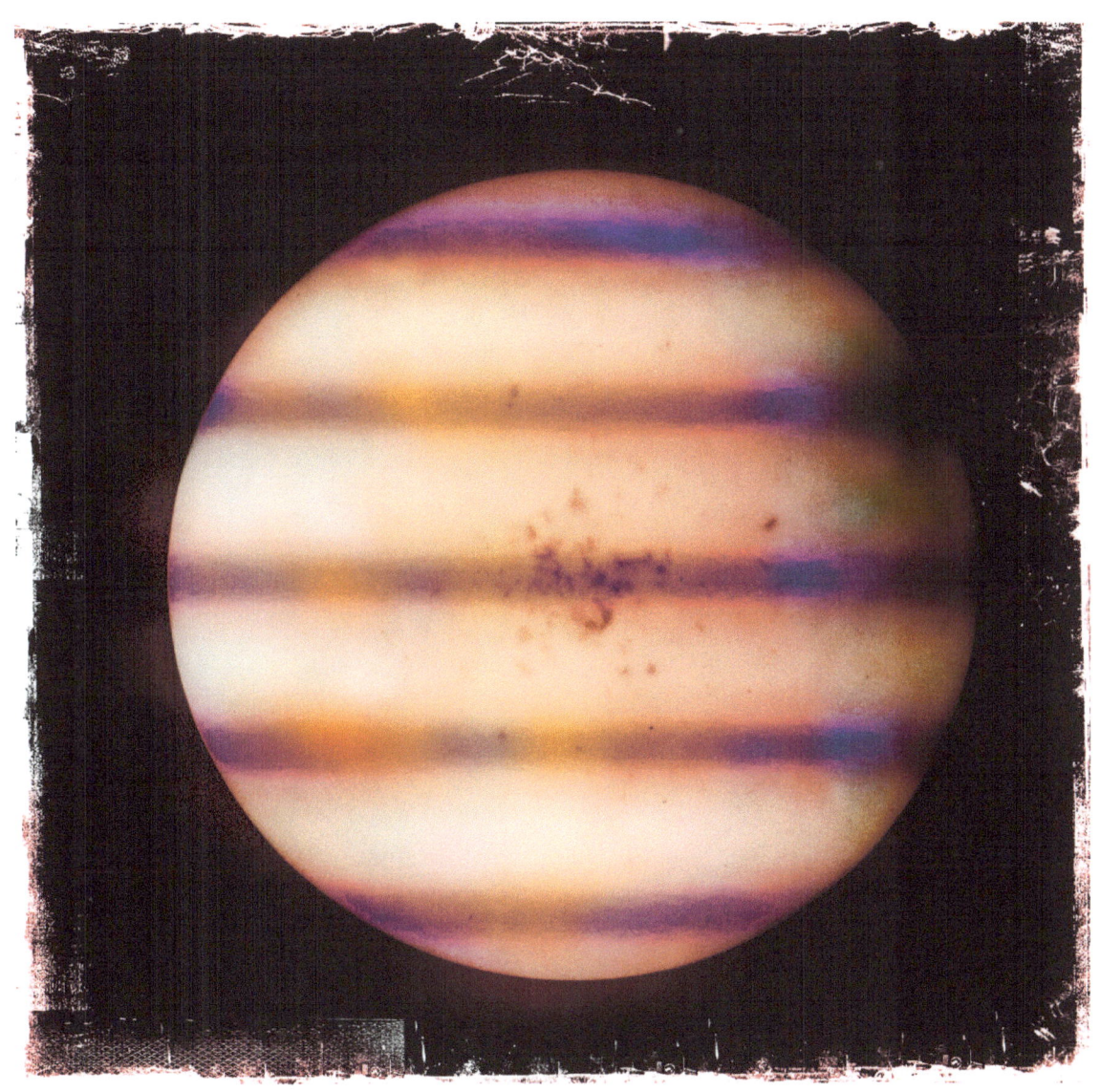

15

There is a common notion that if you spend enough money on a camera, you don't need to know anything. The camera will do it all for you and you will *shoot like a pro*.

Camera makers spend fortunes to propagate this notion. It's the *Same Old* really...

"You press the button, we do the rest" was used by *George Eastman* to sell his first *Kodak* camera in 1888.

The interesting thing is that even when the device does it all for you as does a *Box Brownie* or an *iPhone*, there is still a lot to learn. Not about the techno of the device, but about what makes a photograph work or not. It's about developing what is called the *photographer's eye*.

Lighting contributes as much to photography as nearly everything else put together. One of the core lighting concepts is called the *Family of Angles.*

In plain English, this means if you want a light to shine off something, you have to get the correct angle between the light, the camera and what it is you are photographing.

Below, an overcast sky gives the broadest *family of angles*, but it still does not wrap all the way around the curved edges of the droplet. Here we see reflected treetops.

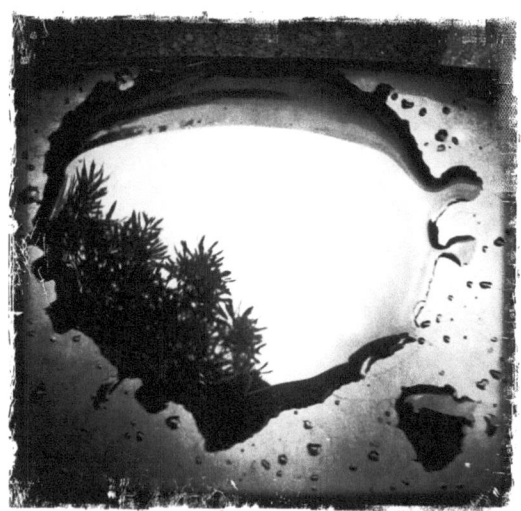

In the image opposite, rain on a glass table is *reflecting* (as distinct from *refracting*) security bars and sky, both happily within our *family of angles*.

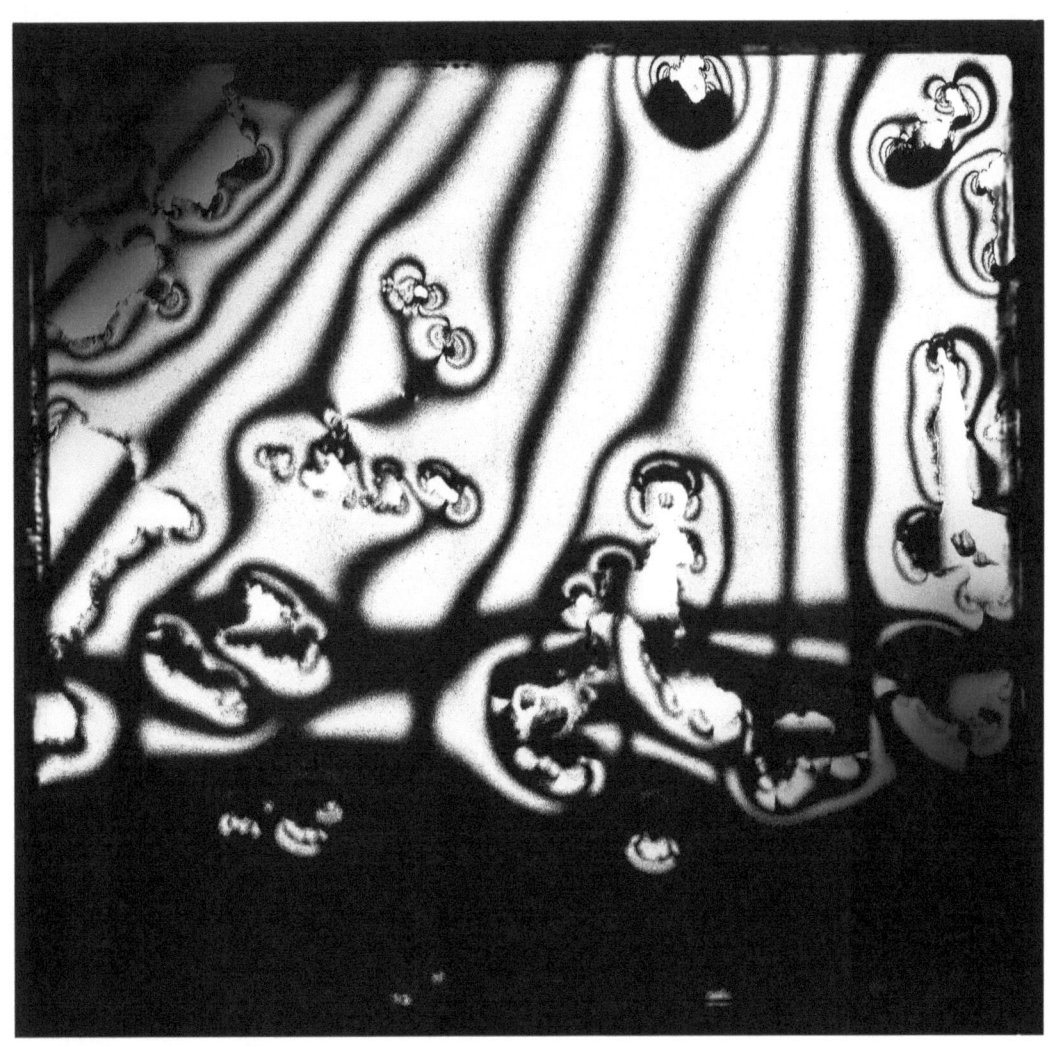

JAN 86

Side Lighting was a new form of lighting used by Renaissance painters such as *Rembrandt* and *Caravaggio*. It is often is referred to as *Rembrandt Lighting*. It creates *modelling*, which emphasises the form and texture of what it illuminates, in this case my face.

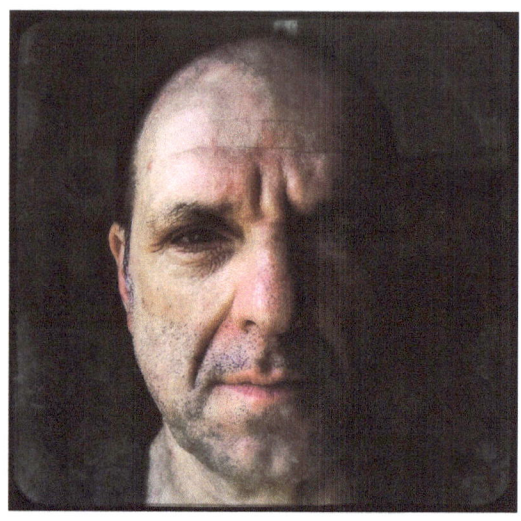

On the beach is a stone that to me resembles a *Fertility Figurine*. The lighting, just on sunset, articulates the form of this stone. It also accentuates its texture and that of the sand.

Interestingly, if this stone were a person, this angle of lighting is like that in the *middle of the day*. A very old "rule" of photography is "do *not photograph in the middle of day*". This time is reserved for *mad dogs and Englishmen,* and of course photographers who do not know better.

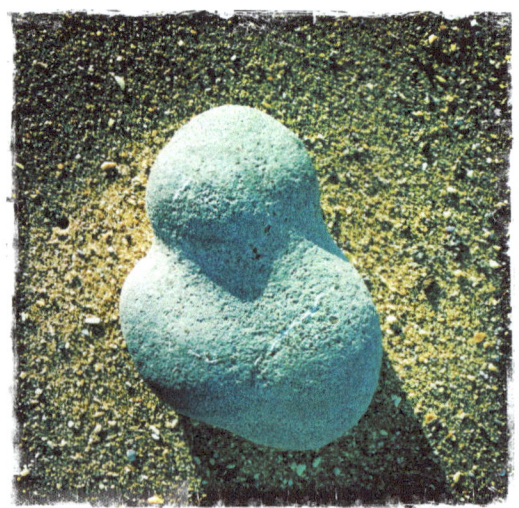

The lighting of the pigeons provides a sense of depth largely created by the shadows on the nearer wall.

Cameras do not provide lighting, they record it.

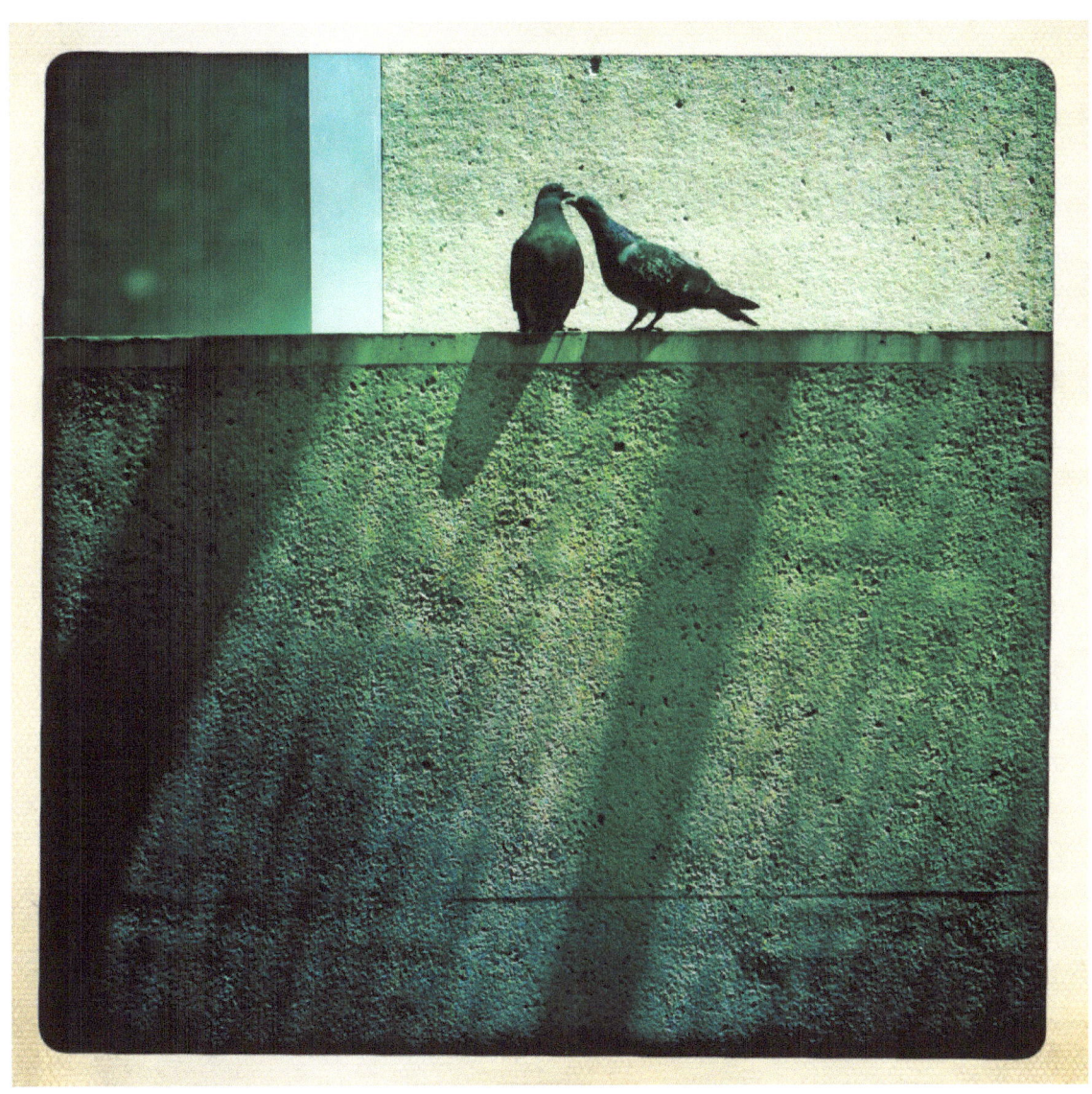

Daylight has the remarkable quality of being absolutely even over the entire planet, except of course when there are clouds, shadows, twilight and night.

In our built environments, we often find variations in the intensity of the light. These are often the nemesis of good *exposure* (do not ever stand a bride in the sun and a groom in the shade), but on occasions, lighting variations become the subject of photographs in themselves.

Sometimes the ordinary, a counter top refrigerated drink cabinet in the case of the image overleaf, becomes a stunning play of light *refracting* through bottles and water droplets.

In advertising photography, creating this image deliberately would take a crew a day. They would use cheats such as glycerine or splattered polyester resin. Here, what luck, all I have had to do was notice it, point and *press the button*.

The spirit of the *Box Brownie* is alive and well.

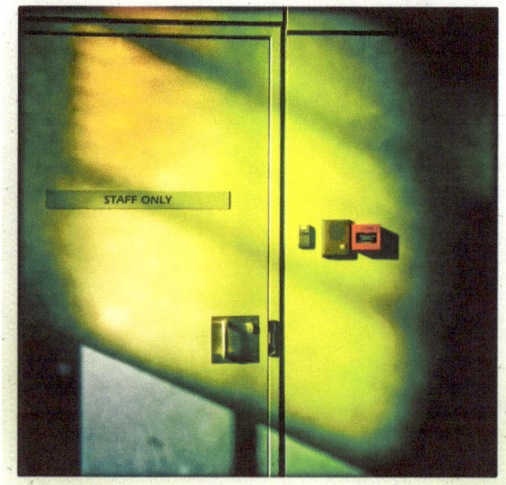

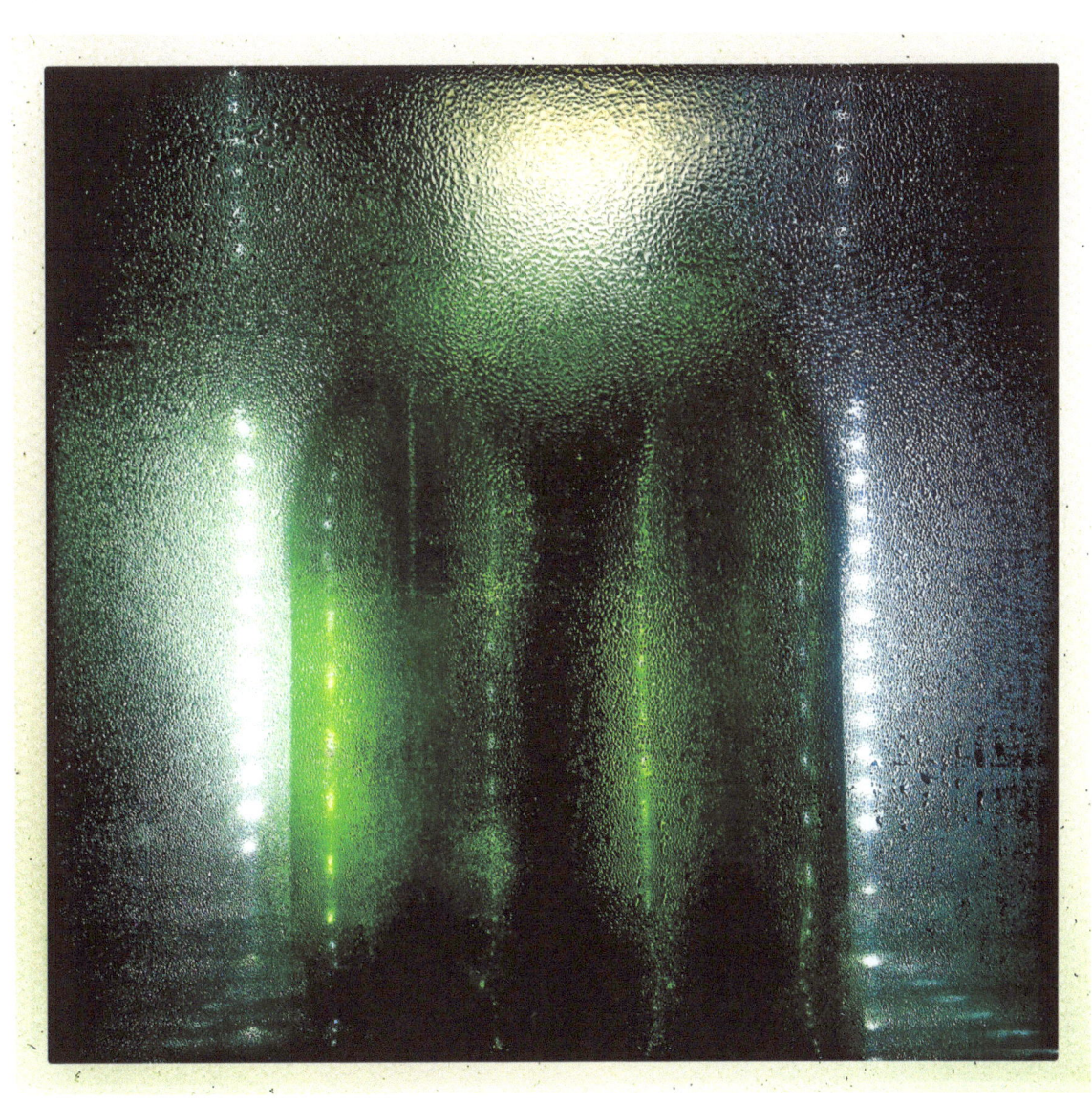

81

16

Strays

The dogs here are not strays. "Strays" refers to my inability to put everything into a neat and tidy category without any orphans. Here are my photographic orphans.

One aspect of photographing dogs, or anything else for that matter, is it is rarely necessary to photograph things in their entirety. In fact there is no such thing as a photograph where everything in the picture is photographed in its entirety.

There is always a *dark side of the Moon.*

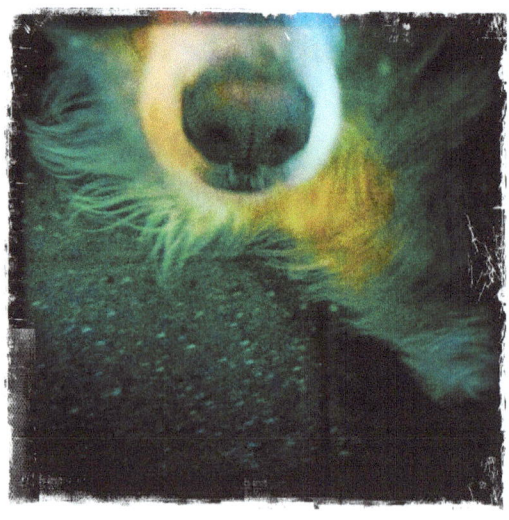

In photography, placement of the edge of the photograph is one of the most fundamental decisions the photographer makes.

Where on the Earth, literally, do you place the edges of your photograph? What you include or exclude and how you arrange what is in-frame, tells as much about you, the photographer, as it does about what you think you are telling us about your subject.

What is remarkable is that even an image of part of a dog reads to us as dog. *Gestalt Perception* is a field of study which tries to understand how humans convert light rays into shapes, symbols, things and meaning. Even the nose of a dog (left) is dog to us.

The dog on the right has a nose for *composition*. His nose is right on the *Golden Mean* both horizontally and vertically. Two *Golden Means*, one photograph, one nose. More about *composition* and the *Golden Mean* later.

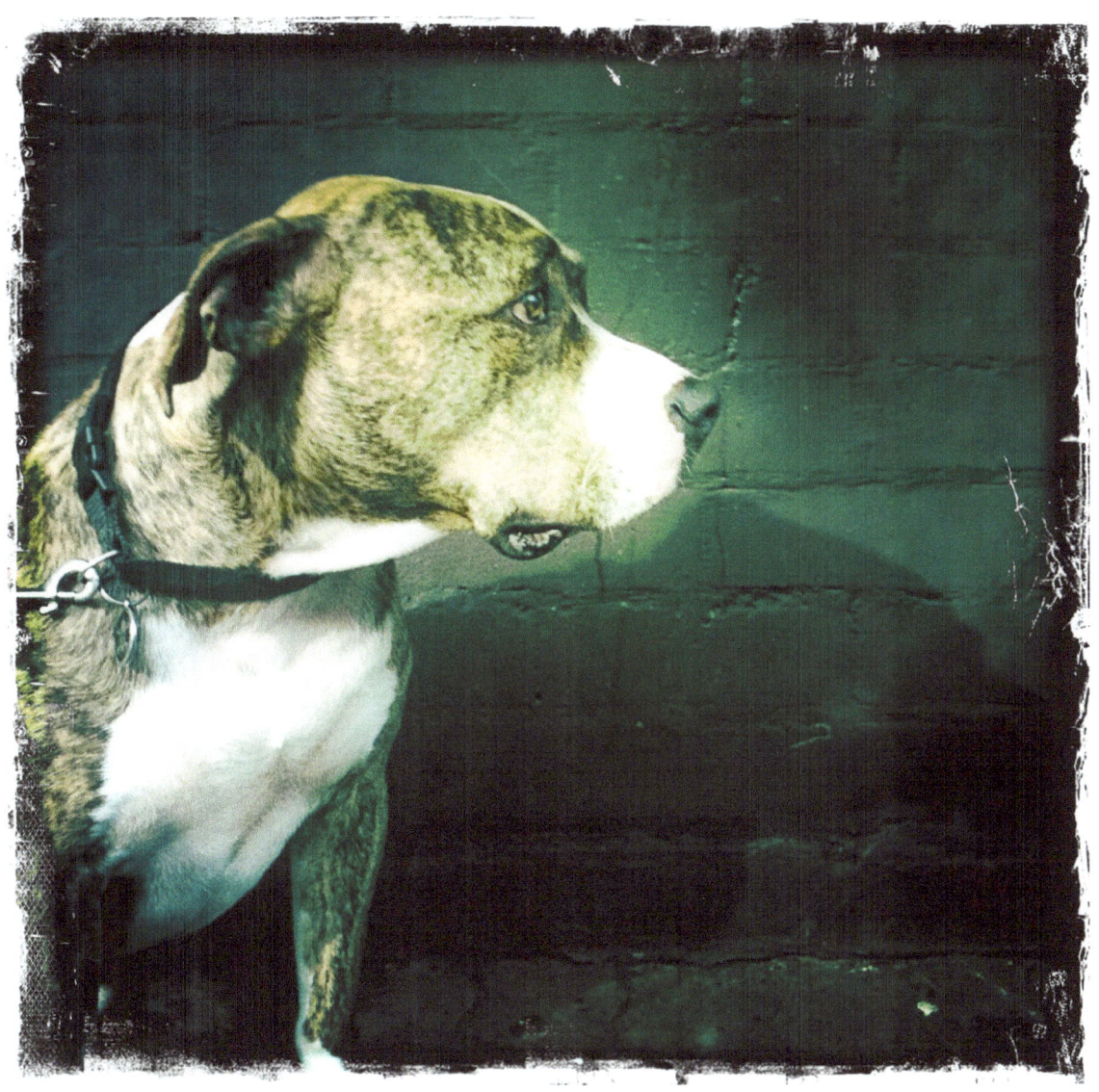

The saying "*Less is More*" dates back to 1855. It's about painters using less visual information to tell their story, rather than dissipating it in a flurry of irrelevant visual distraction.

It's like music, the best way to hear a sound is when there is silence, except for the one sound you want to hear.

I used *Silhouette* to simplify, as the outlines of the razor wire and gate are readily recognisable. Following recognition, we begin to assemble a story and to pose questions.

Without a foreground or detail on the gate, the clouds offer just enough information to say photograph rather than ink drawing over watercolour wash. So we are dealing with reality, are we not?

You tell me: does this photograph communicate locked in or locked out? Your answer will have much more to do with your own psychology than the photograph itself.

There is only separation by gate and razor wire, but why?

Is it the view of someone inside a refugee camp, plucked from a sinking boat? On the other hand, the view of a person who takes one last look back from a prison escape? Or how the utility company attempts to protect infrastructure that powers a city, from a terrorist attack?

Is the gate even locked? We cannot see a padlock or locking mechanism. If you say either yes or no, you are damned for making an assumption. Your brain is writing a story from your own internal library of stories, creating its own *semiotic play*.

The meaning to be read from nearly all photographs has as much to do with the viewer as the photographer. Unless there is a *Caption*.

Captions tell the viewer how to interpret a photograph: they anchor it. This has long been understood in traditional media.

Social Media now also embraces *#captions* wholeheartedly.

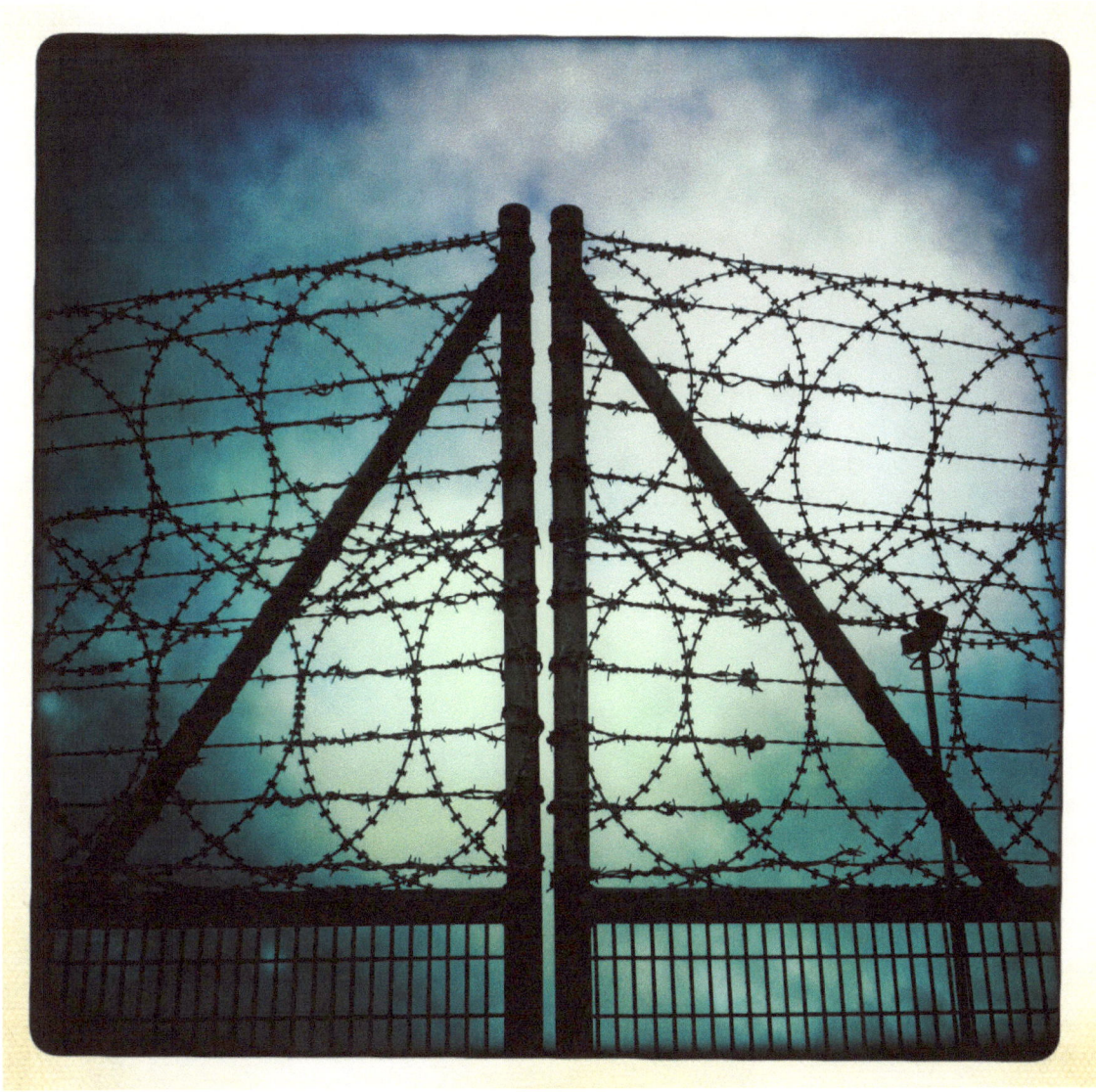

This caption provides no information at all about the photograph or its context. This may well annoy you as you I am sure you were expecting something informative to be written here.

I included these bicycle photos as they are about *line* and shape and *photographic point of view*, remember our pal, *Rodchenko?*

How low to the ground and how close to the passing feet was I to get the shot overleaf? If you stand, you will always get a standing view of the world. Why limit yourself?

I only wanted to share three bicycle photos so I've included a photograph of droplets on a red petrol pony to match the red bicycle. The pony is a *Mustang*.

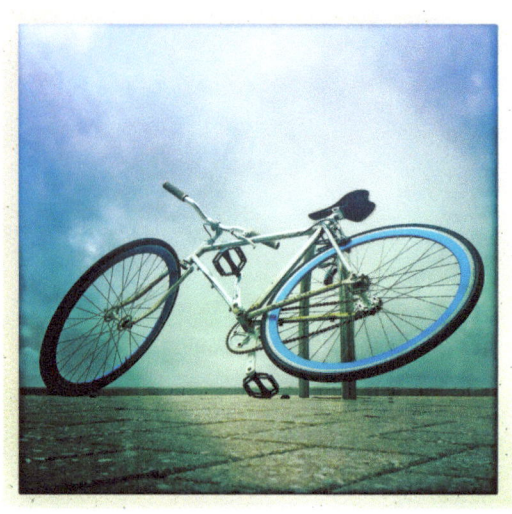

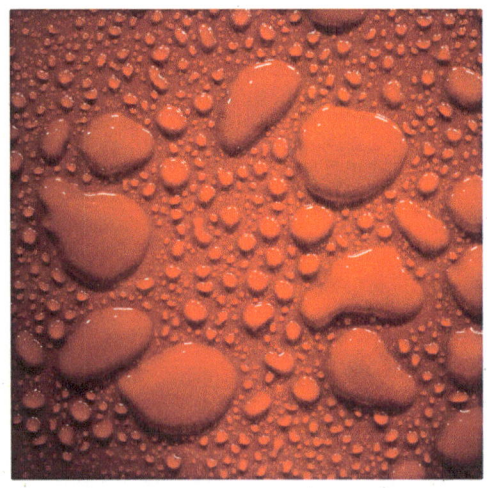

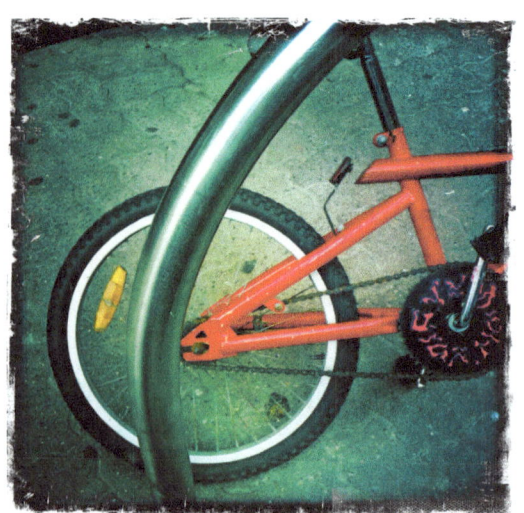

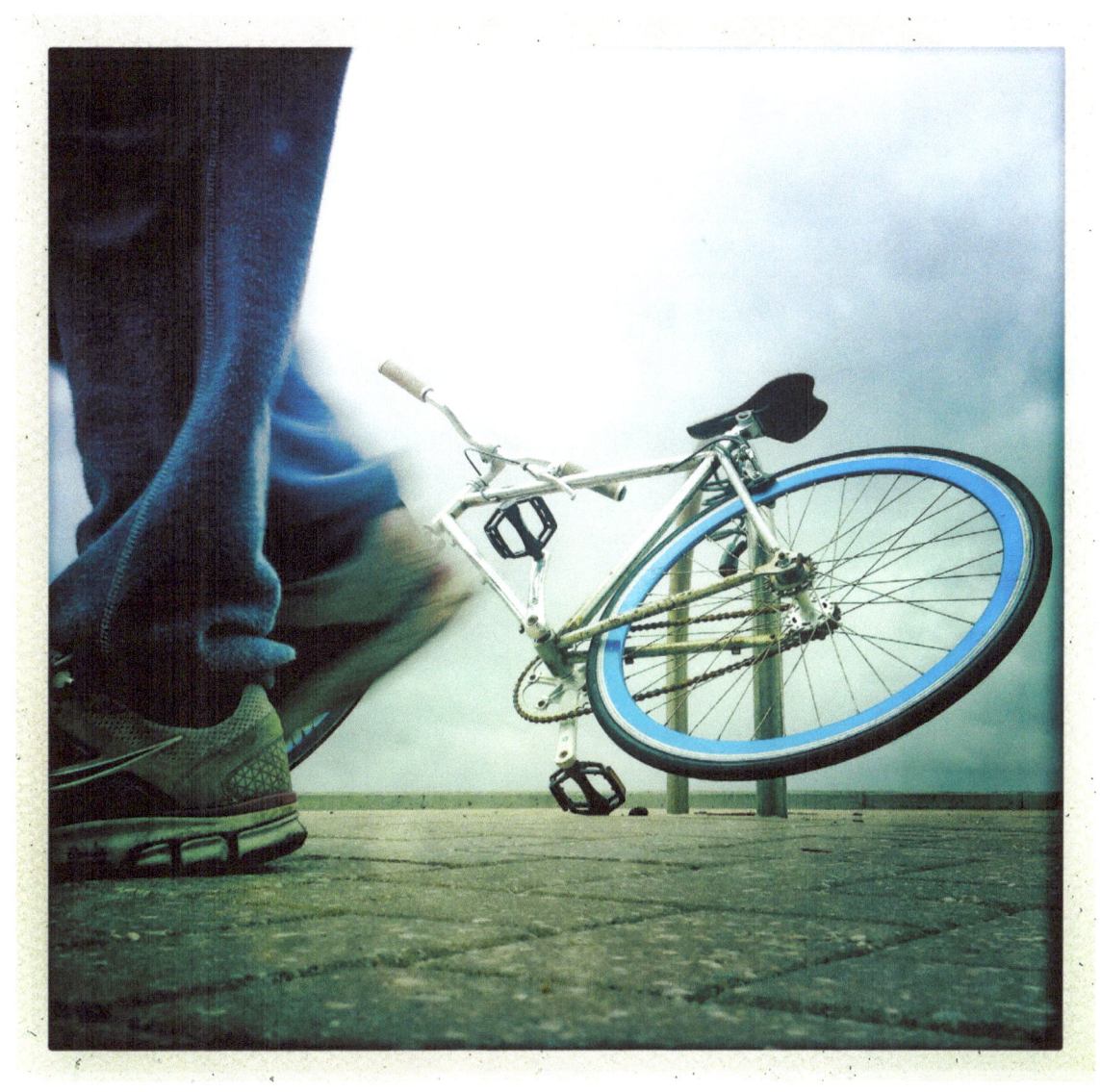

Photography has a remarkable ability to record oddities, things we do not see because we are looking only at what our *mental filters* let us see.

Image opposite. It is peak hour in a city train station and I respond to the form of the train window. Back at the computer, with some time, I discover a *surreal landscape* at play within the frame of this train window.

There is a clock tower on a timber structure on which small figures stand. It is 3:00 and a child jester on a throne is wearing a banana hat. I have unknowingly recorded a *surreal* arcane urban landscape that has no existence outside this photograph.

With this image, I am a *Surrealist* photographer. I am seeing an image like one of *Ian Miller's* disturbingly dark *Green Dog Trumpet* illustrations.

The way the camera has rendered and assembled the image could be argued as representing what was actually there. It can all be explained scientifically, but I just don't see things scientifically.

A camera is more objective and truthful than our own perception. It MUST photograph what is there according to its settings, lens and other parameters. It has no choice.

When we say that the camera does not record reality, we would be more accurate in saying that we do not see reality while blaming the camera for the observed differences.

The photographer must understand and explore what each camera does, how this differs from human perception, and then exploit the similarities and differences.

Place a pen tip on any word on this page and look at it. Without moving your eyes from the pen tip, how many words either side can you read? If you can read more than two or three either side you are moving your eyes.

A camera would see all words on the page equally in one photograph, you have to move your eyes. This is only the first of the demonstrations on differences I use when teaching.

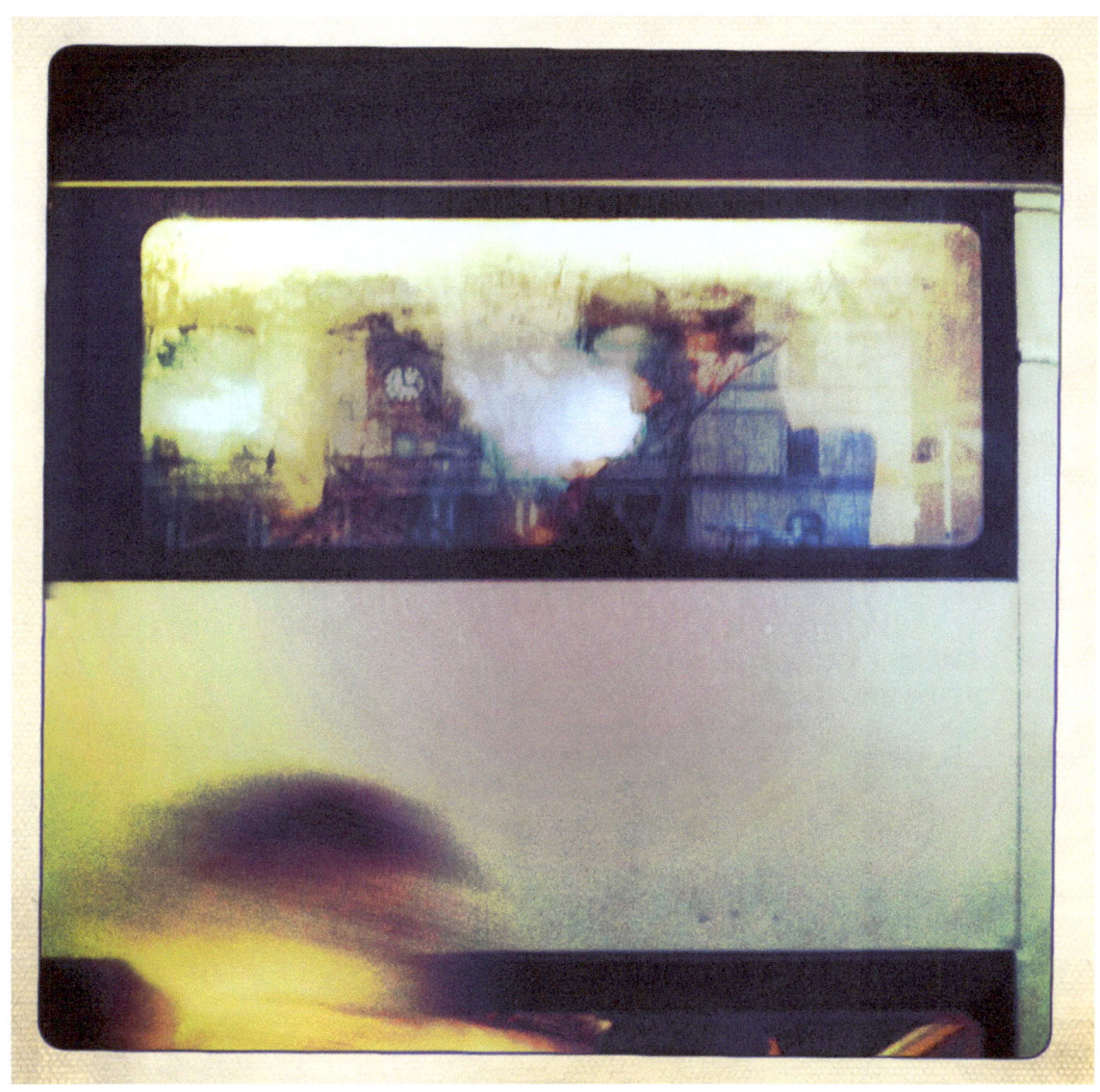

This page is about not taking lazy as an answer and putting in the effort needed to get the best photograph.

While sitting at a cafe with friends a rainbow appeared. All present stay in their seats and pull out their smartphones, myself included. My first photograph was unmemorable.

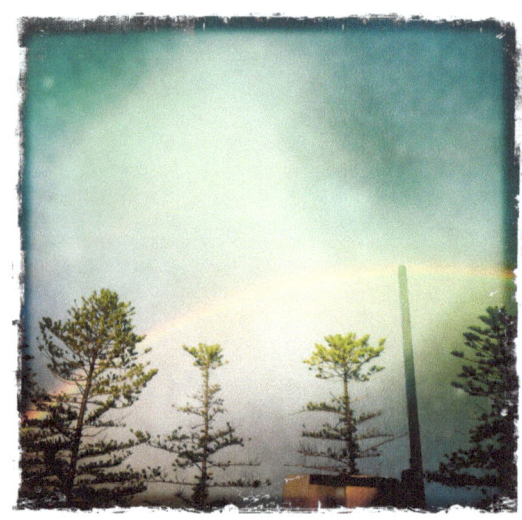

Then I noticed a pipe protruding from a screen and moved to make the rainbow appear to pour out of that pipe. Better and worth the Olympian effort it took to stand up from my comfortable chair. On my third attempt I felt even better about the result.

The story goes there is a *pot of gold at the end of the rainbow*, but have you ever asked from where do rainbows come?

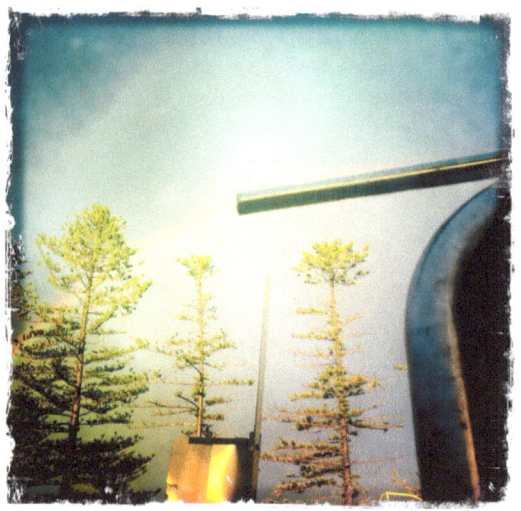

The camera never lies. The reward for my effort is that I am the first person in the world to prove, with my *iPhone* camera, that rainbows come from the little pipe sticking out of a screen at my local cafe.

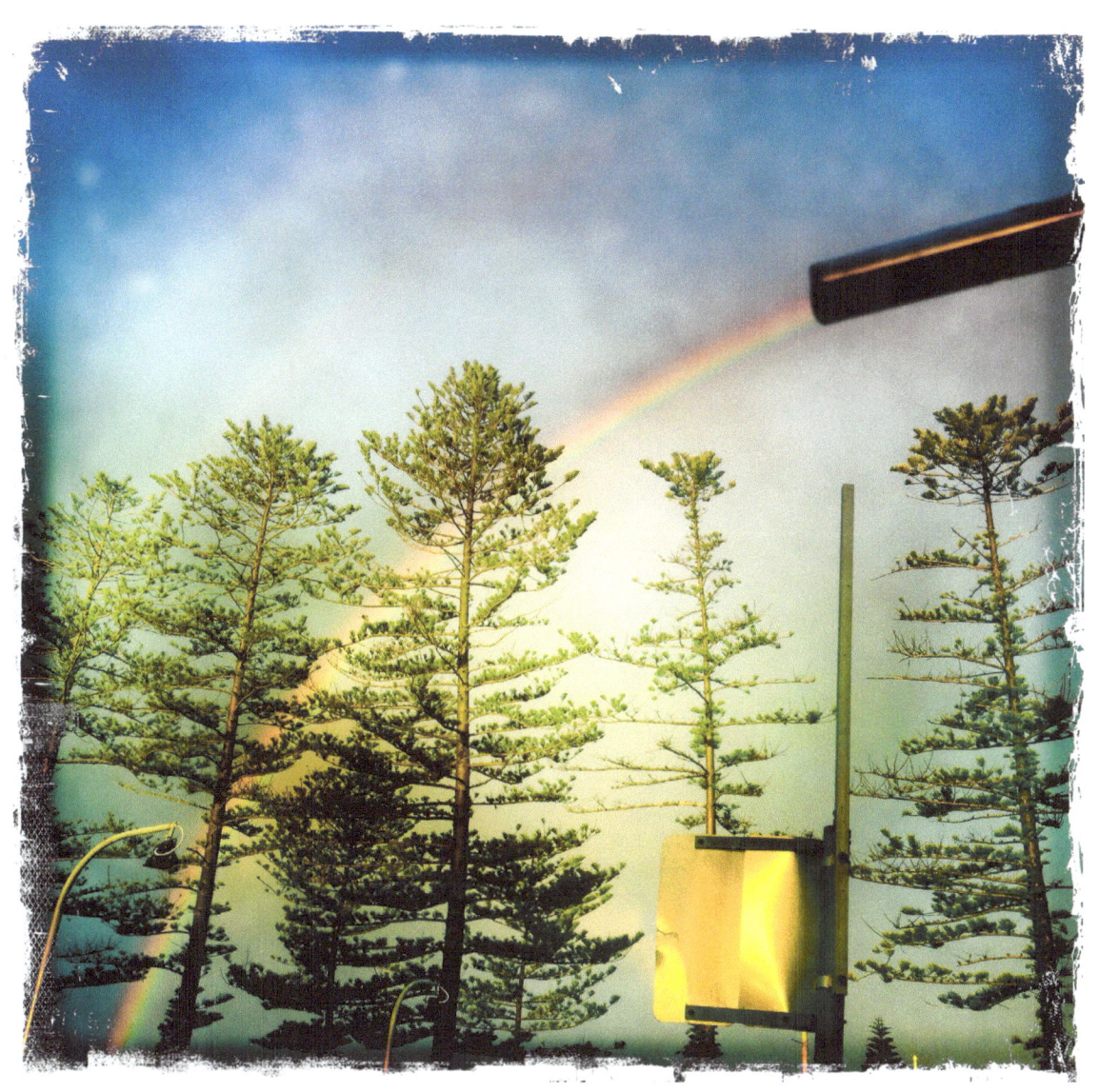

What people write for public consumption is often very strange.

Our cities and lives are so full of writing that if one were allergic to these words, one would surely be deceased. Perhaps something in us has already died and we have not yet noticed.

Only women liked the image opposite, when I posted it to social media. There are gender differences at work here.

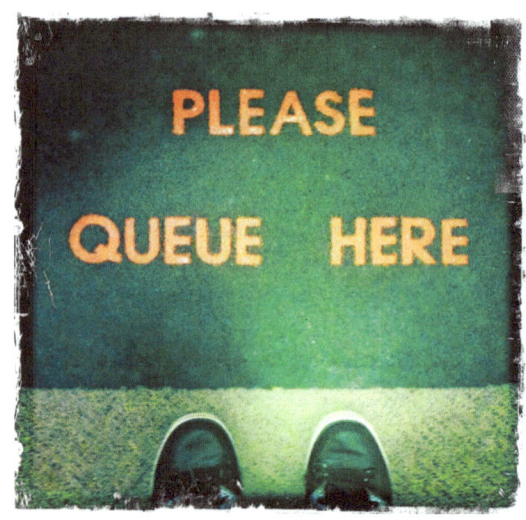

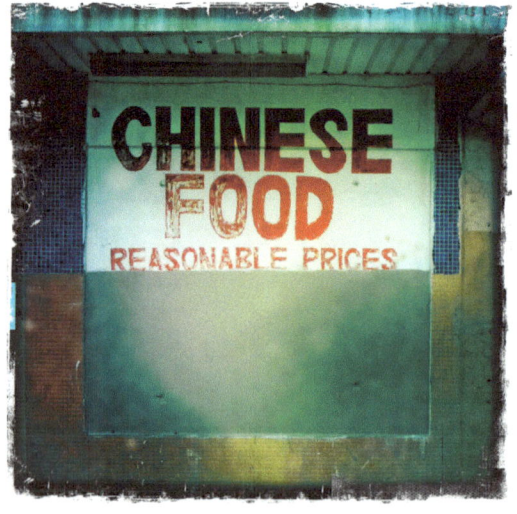

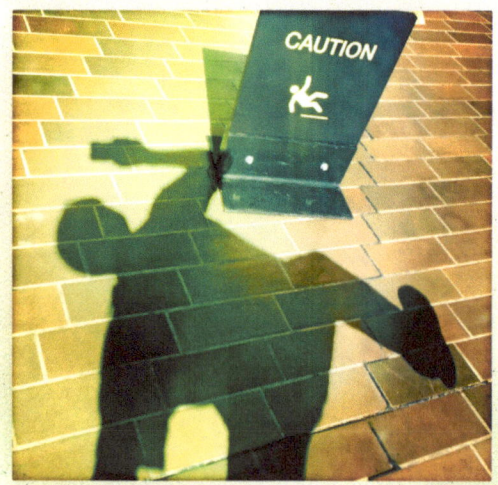

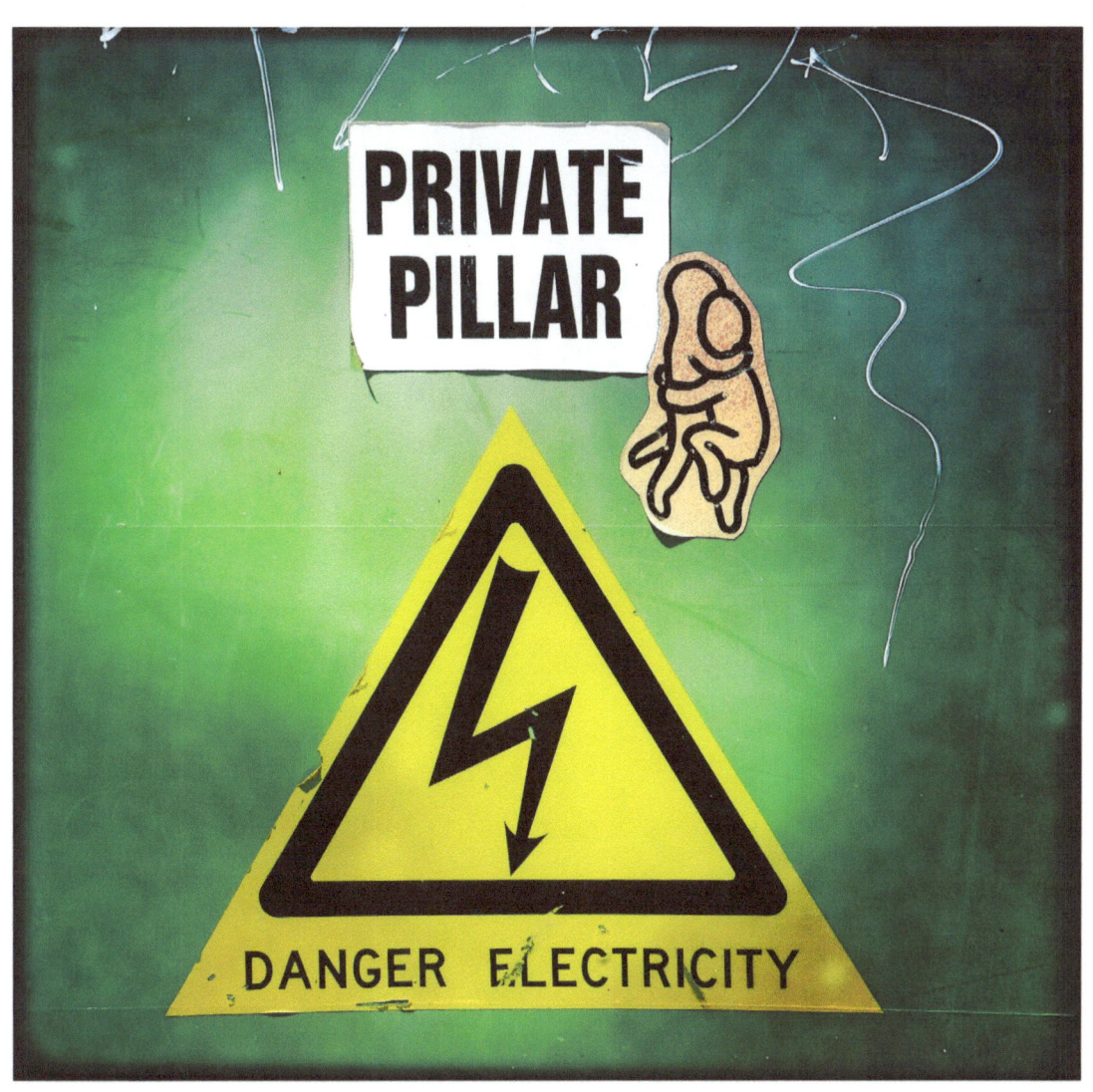

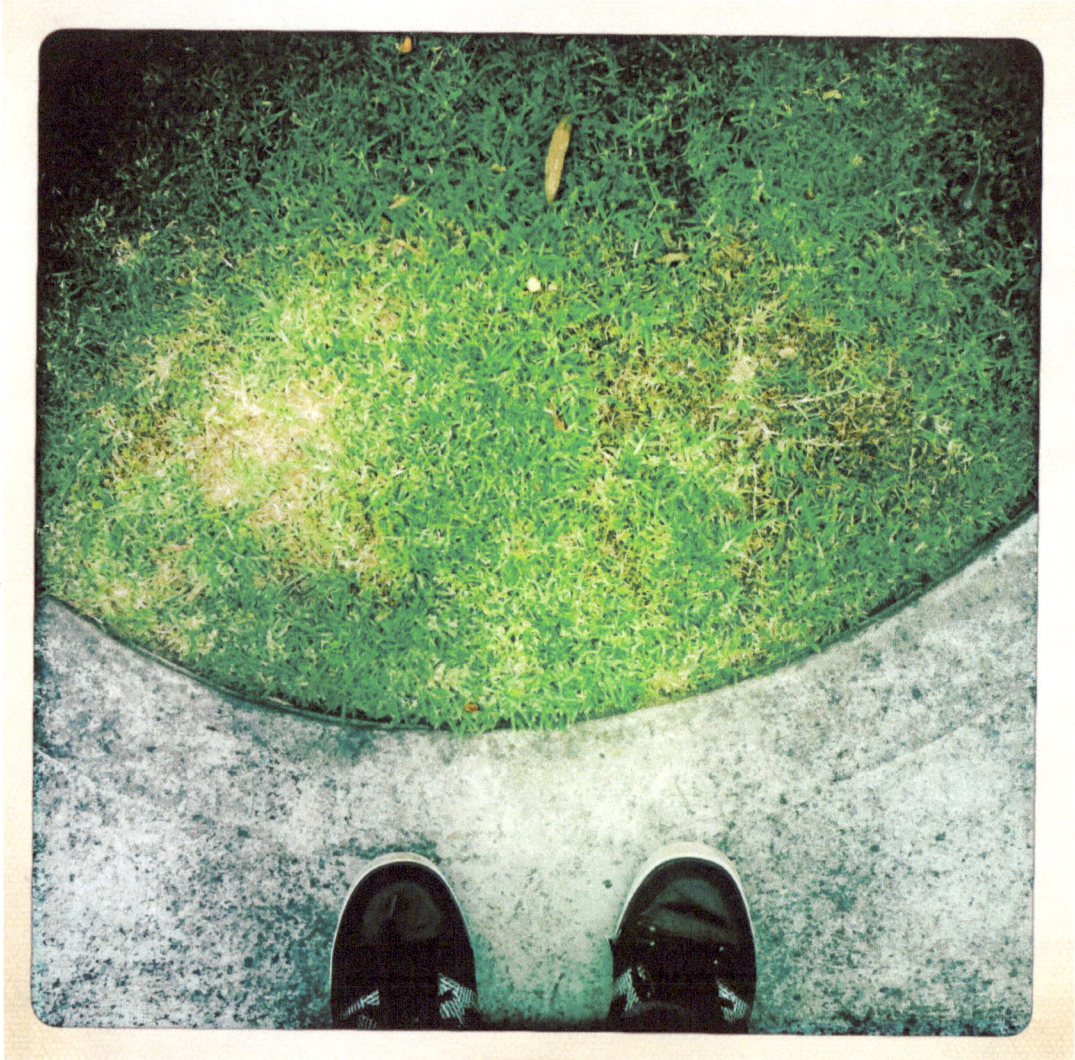

There is no room for my usual text on this page or the next three

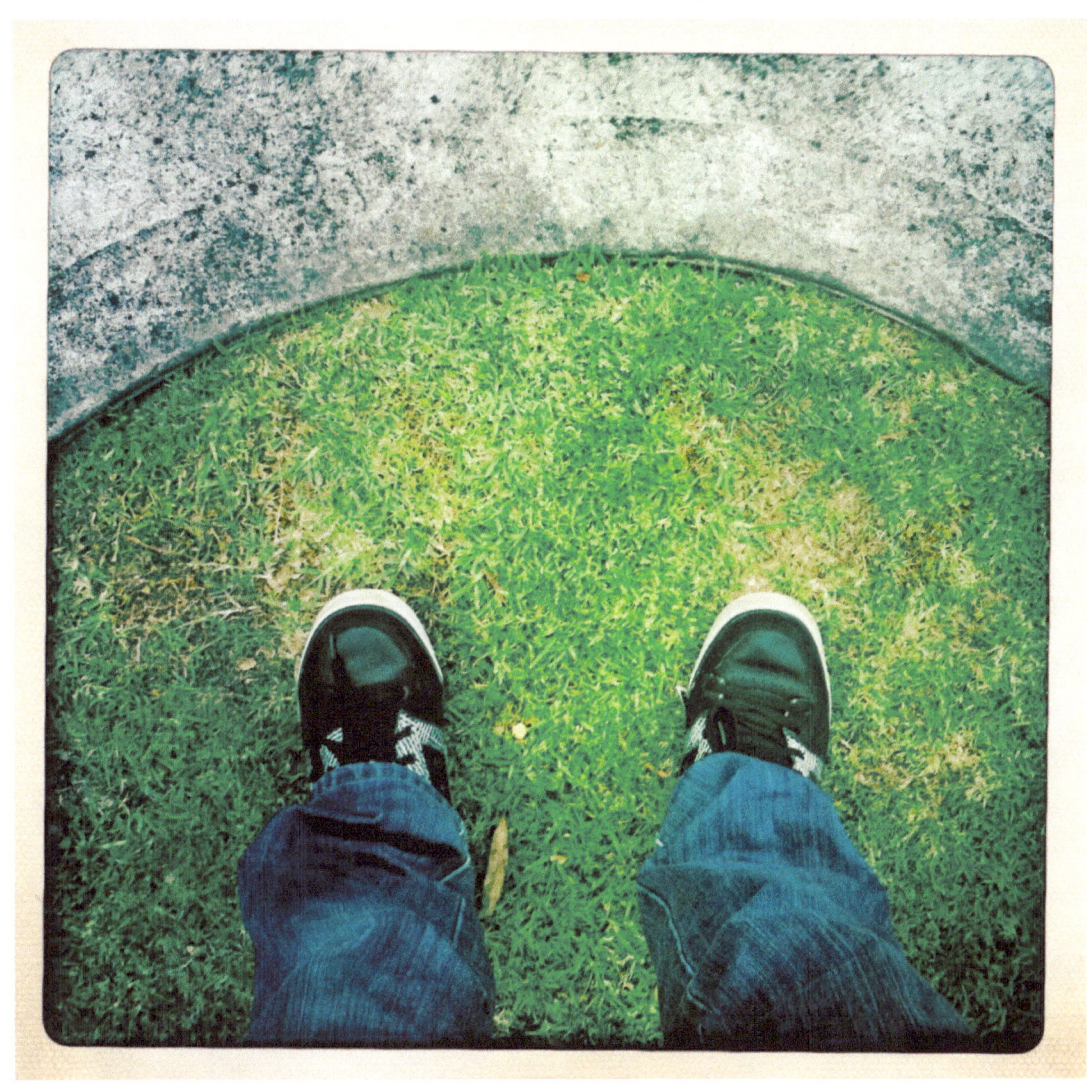

as I was taken by a fit of photographic purism and didn't want

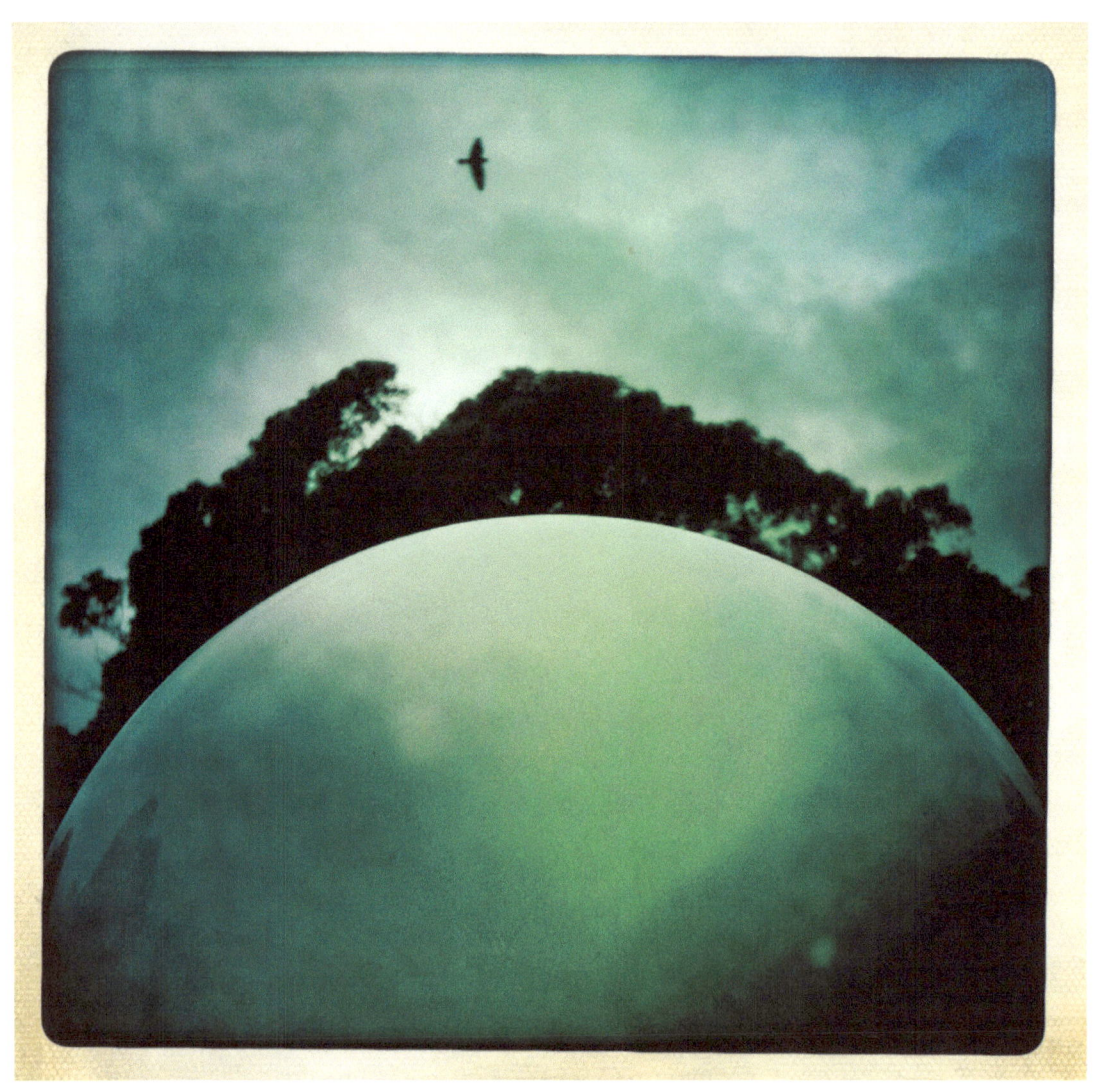

to dilute the purity of my photos with excess text. You might in passing,

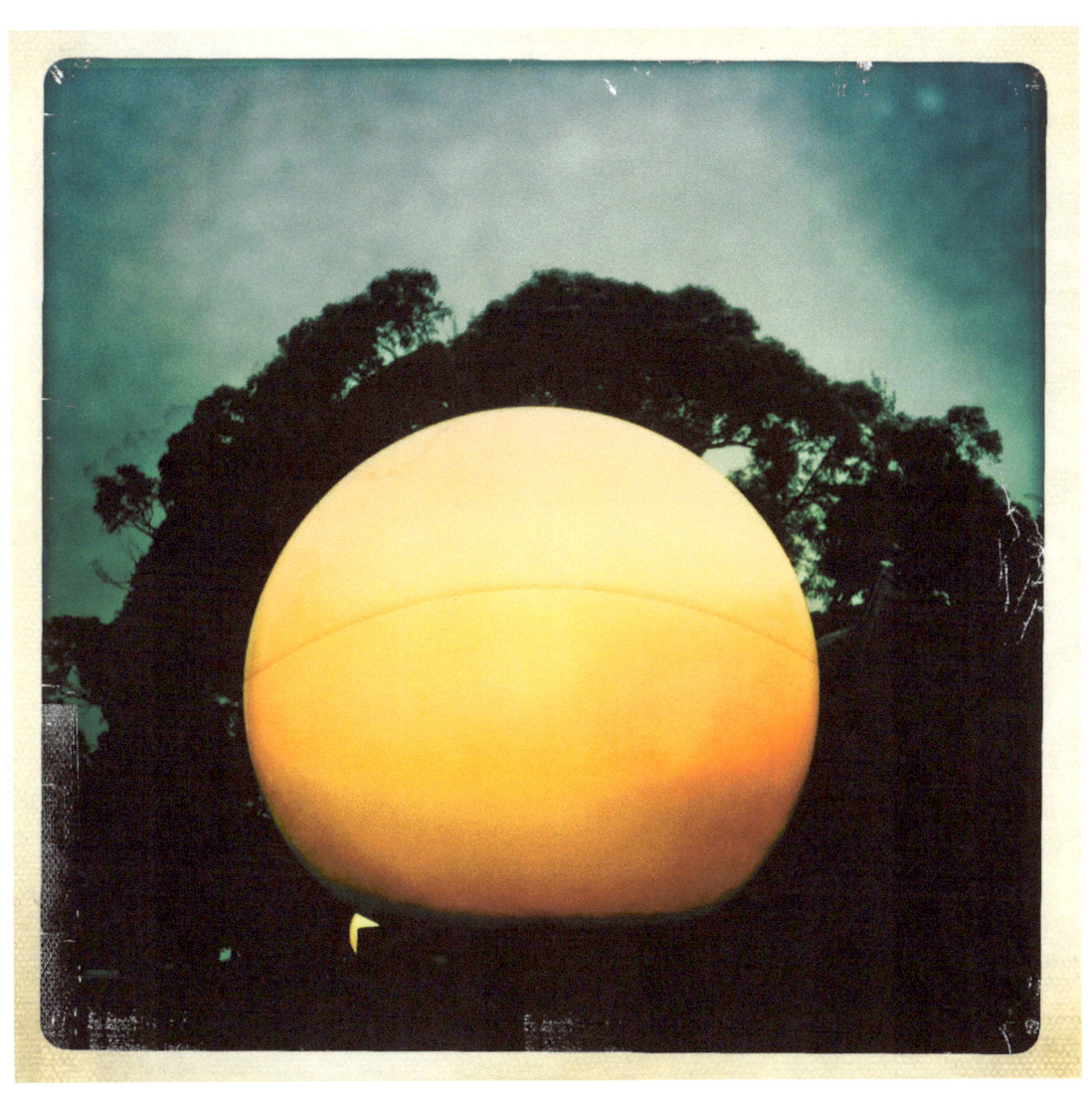

notice the effect of having pairs of related photographs side by side.

18

Old Tricks

This is an old trick, it's an image full of *pattern* and *repetition*. This trick was used by the photography studio *Hipgnosis* and they acknowledged they were not the first in the line to use this trick.

The nice thing about old tricks, or at least the good old tricks, is they can be endlessly used and reused and reused. Unless you mess it up, they will always look good.

Smart devices, have a programmed in aversion to old tricks, so, you have to re-badge the old as the new.

The photograph of the man in Tweed, an old trick, is now a new trick as I used a clever app on a clever phone and included it in a book about *iPhones.*

You might not be able to *teach an old dog a new trick*, but you can teach a new dog an old trick.

The streetscape below is another old trick that uses *perspective* and plenty of *pattern* and *repetition*. Using B&W, a truly old trick, simplifies photographs by eliminating often distracting and unnecessary colour.

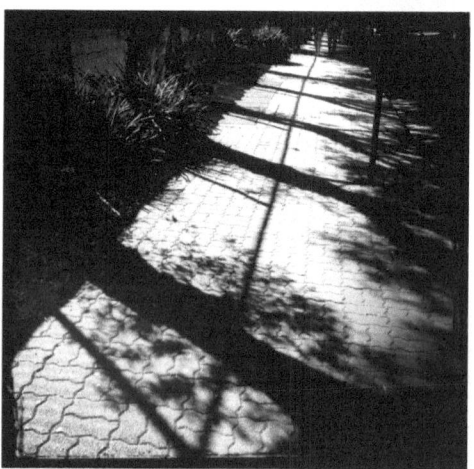

APR 84

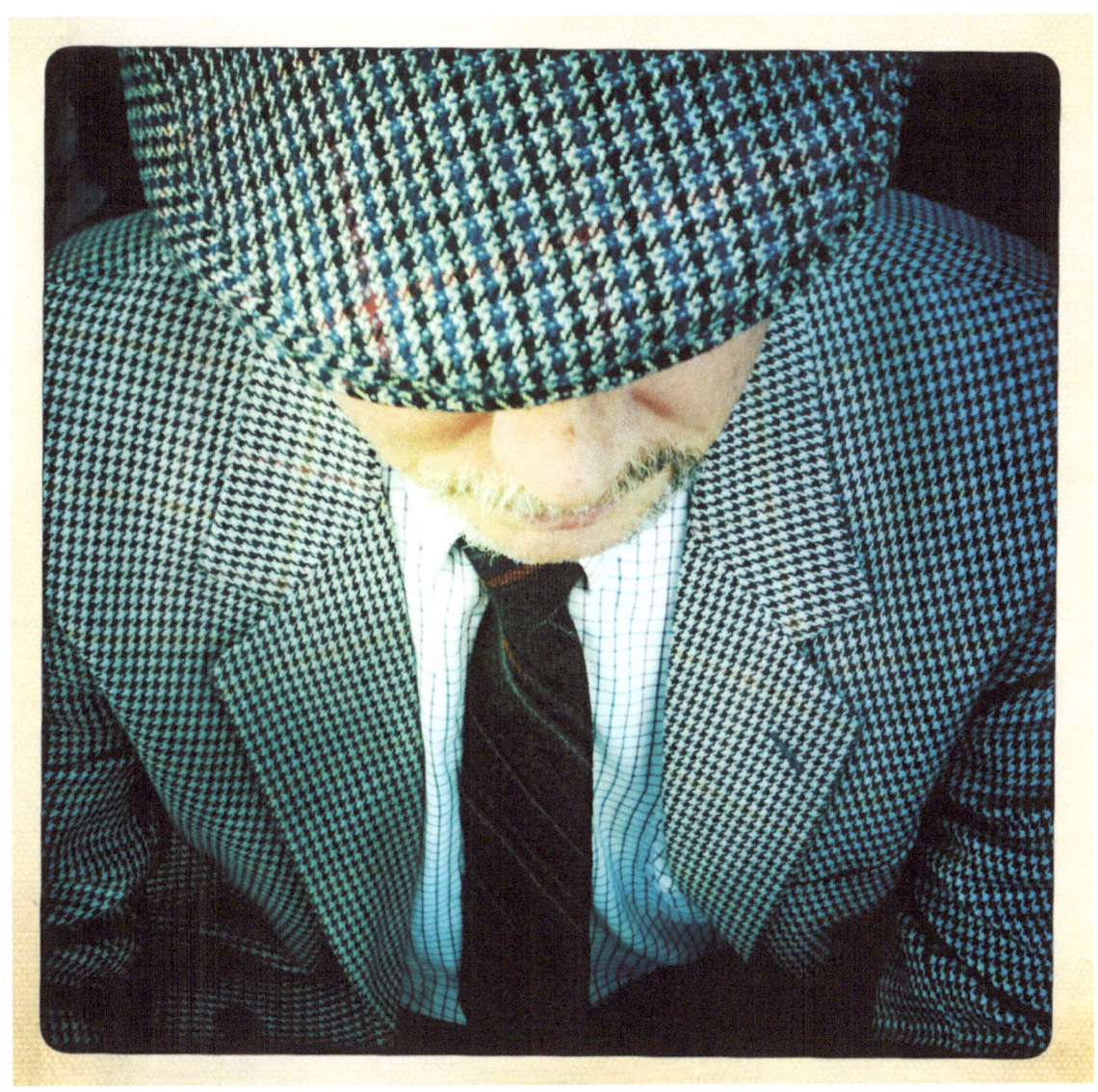

19

Composition

There are *rules of composition* that are not really rules at all. *Ansel Adams* said, "*There are no rules for good photographs, there are only good photographs.*" But rules do work enough of the time for us to take notice of them.

The *Rule of Thirds* is the best known. Divide the picture into thirds and place something on one of the lines or an intersection of the lines. Easy. Many cameras have *thirds* lines on the viewfinder. These might save you from the worst but never guarantee a great photograph.

My attempt, bottom of this page, to create a *Rule of Thirds* image with everything on a third has failed. Only one foot managed it and the other is still being decided on by the line umpire. None of the edges of the yellow line are on a third.

Things often look like they are on a third but are not when you measure them up. Even with only one foot on a third, the image is helped by avoiding putting the important stuff in the *central* square, which nearly always makes for a *compositional* type called "*boring*".

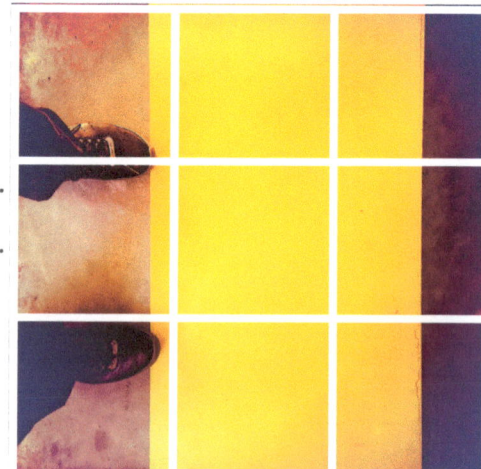

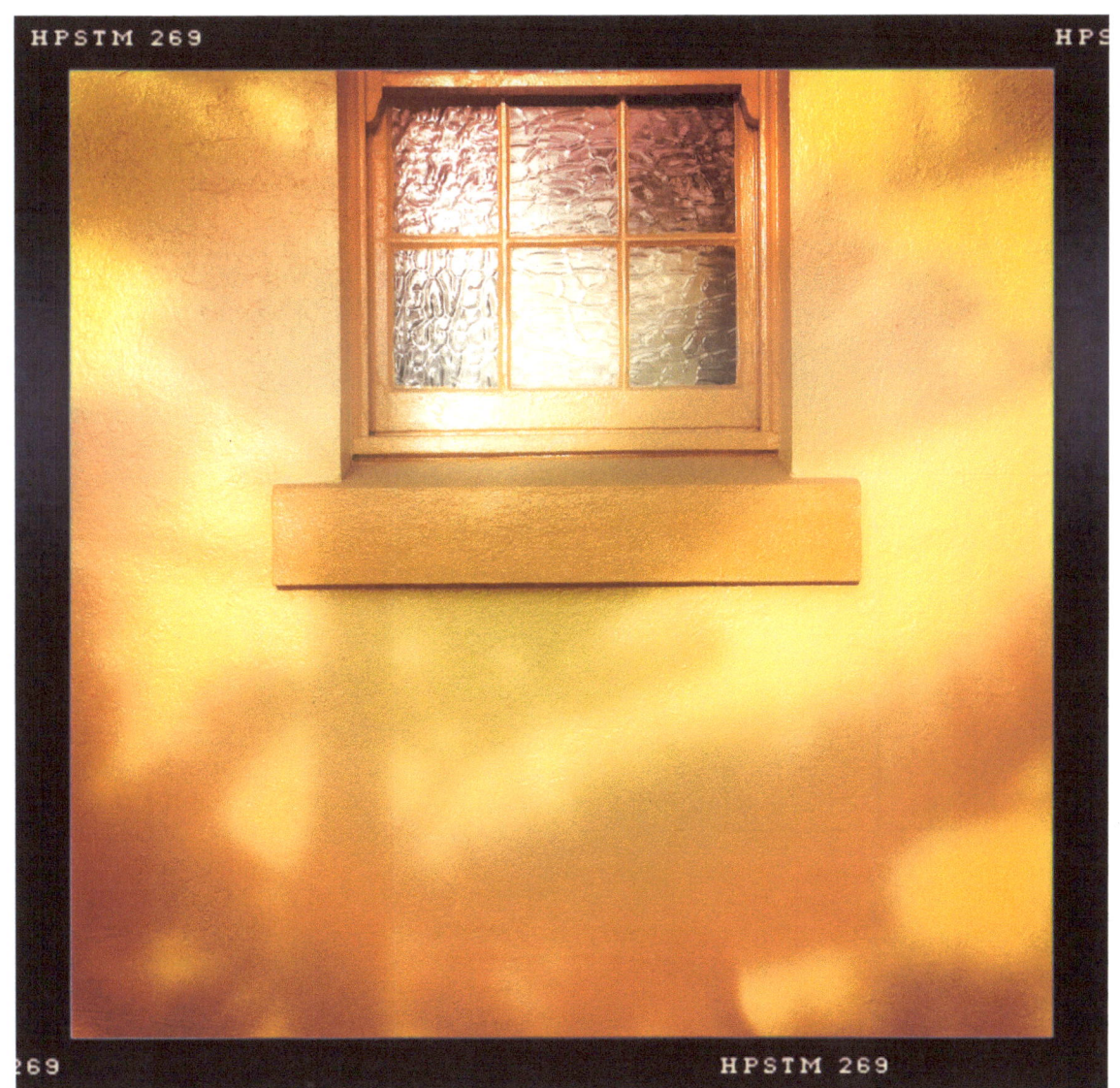

The other big rule is the *Golden Mean*. It is the famously classical Rule and is seen in the dimensions of the *Parthenon* and in many things in nature such as shells and flowers. *Closely related, is the Fibonacci Sequence*, famous for its expression in the *Nautilus shell*.

Some of my photographs match this rule very well. The derivation of the *Golden Mean* is a bit complex and in photography must be done by feel. As a working trick, choose a line or a point somewhere between the middle and a third.

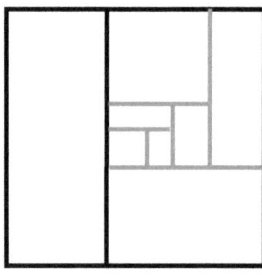

Mathematically the Golden Mean divides an area into two parts with a ratio of roughly 1: 1.618033988749894 848204586834365638117720309179805762862135448622705260462818902449707207204189391374....

A trick with the *Golden Mean* is that once you have divided an image into two parts, you can then keep dividing the divided parts as much as you want, again and again.

The next two spreads show *Rule of Thirds* and *Golden Mean* divisions applied to the same images.

The funny thing is that some images obey BOTH *Thirds* and *Golden Mean* Rules. And some really work well as *compositions* but stick a finger up to both.

Whenever I measure up photographs like this, I am surprised how some images refuse to conform and how some are total slaves to the *Rules*.

This for me only happens AFTER I have taken the photograph. When I am taking a photograph I do not have the time for this sort of analysis.

For me, Rules are a "*B Plan*" to use in the absence of having a better idea at the time. While rules deliver good photographs, brilliance requires us to go beyond using formulae.

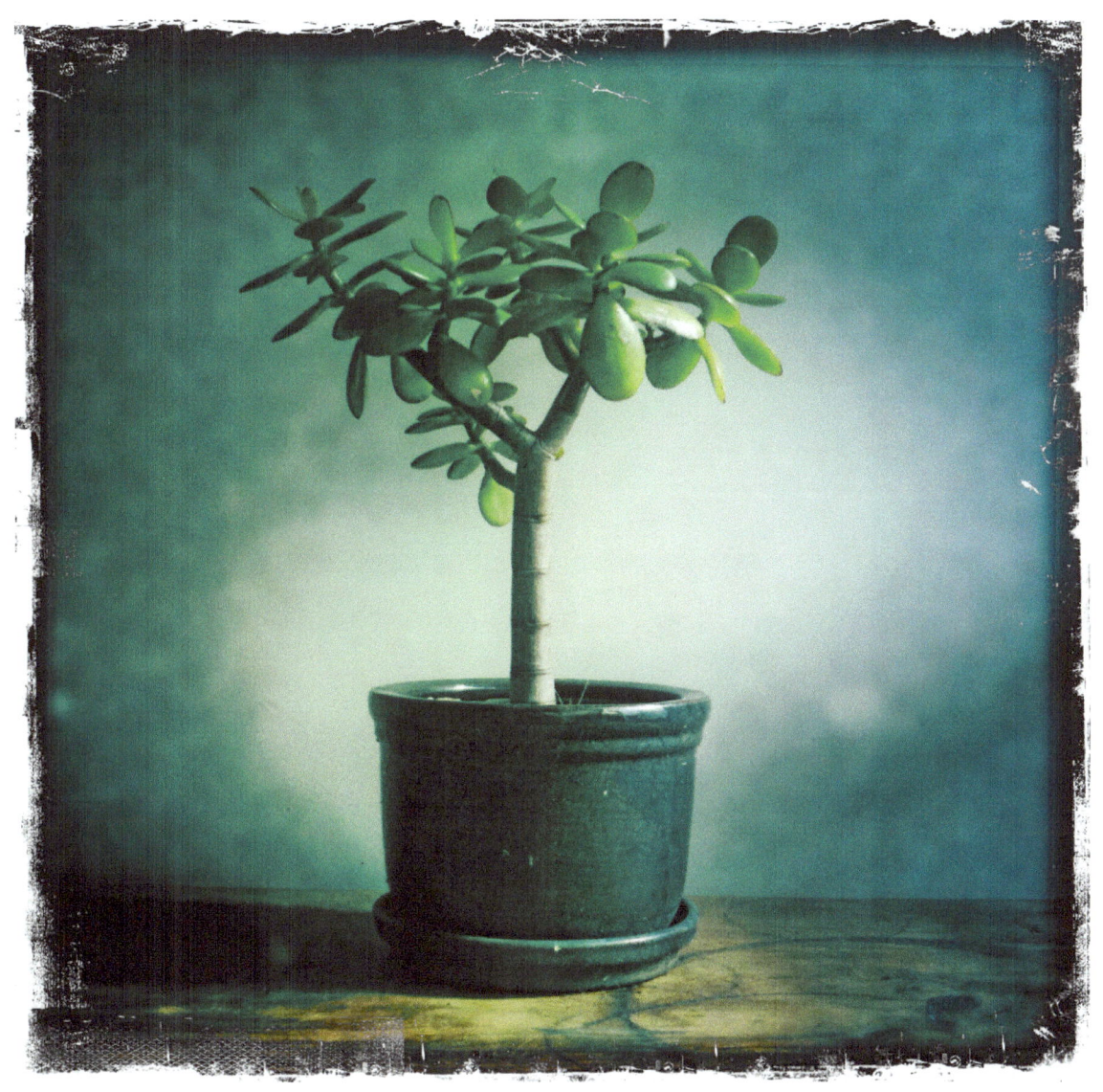

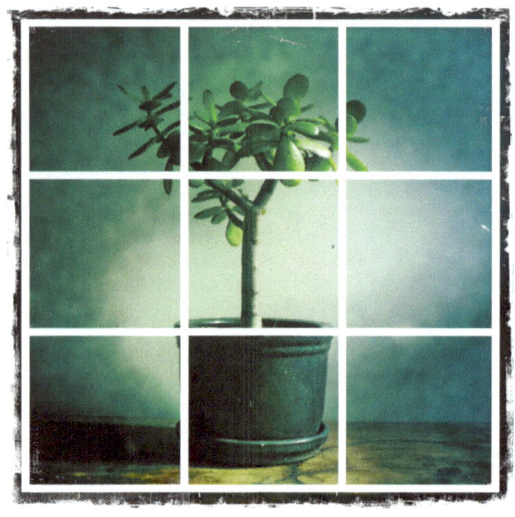
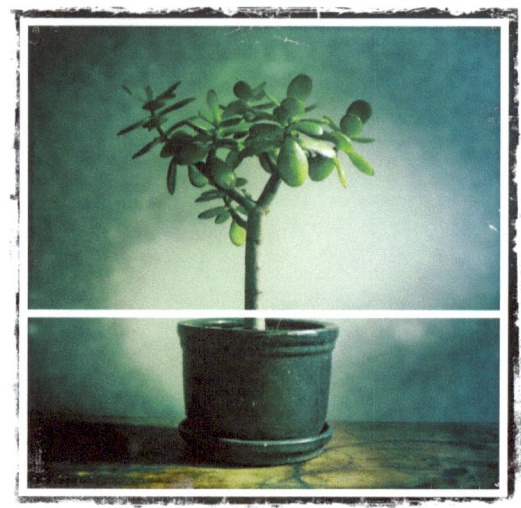
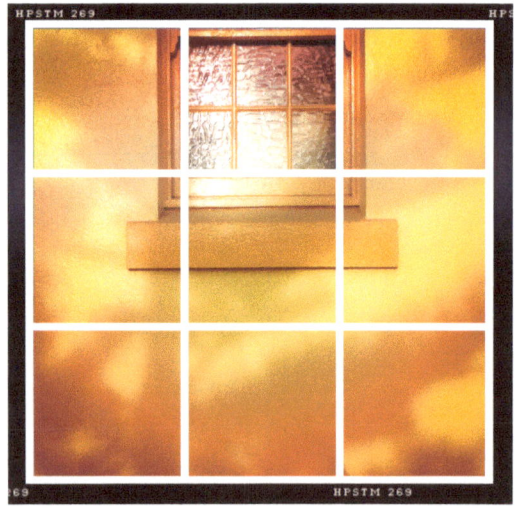
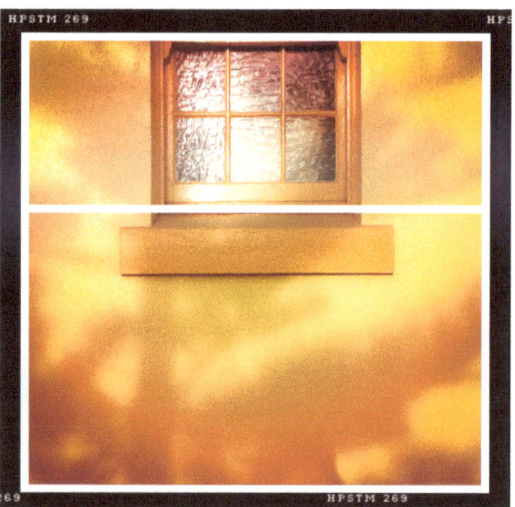

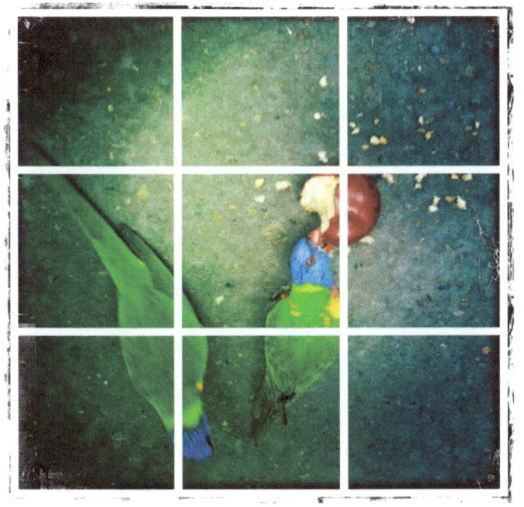
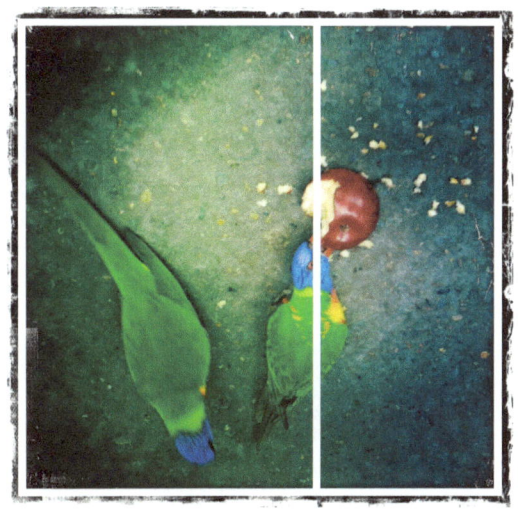
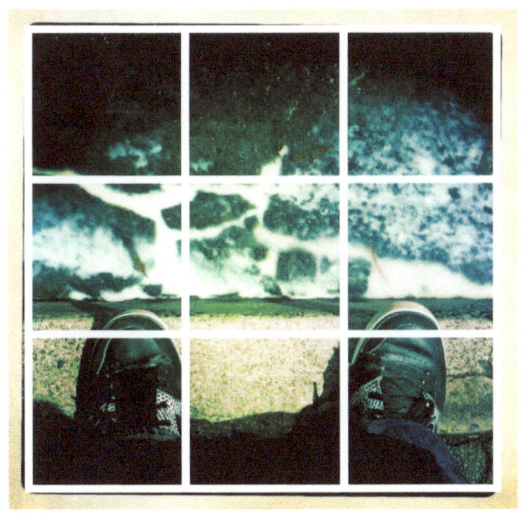
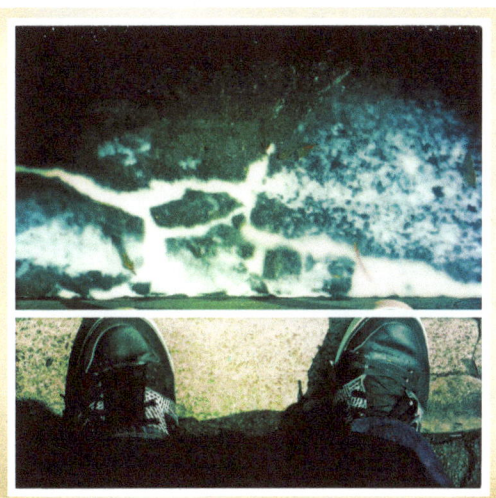

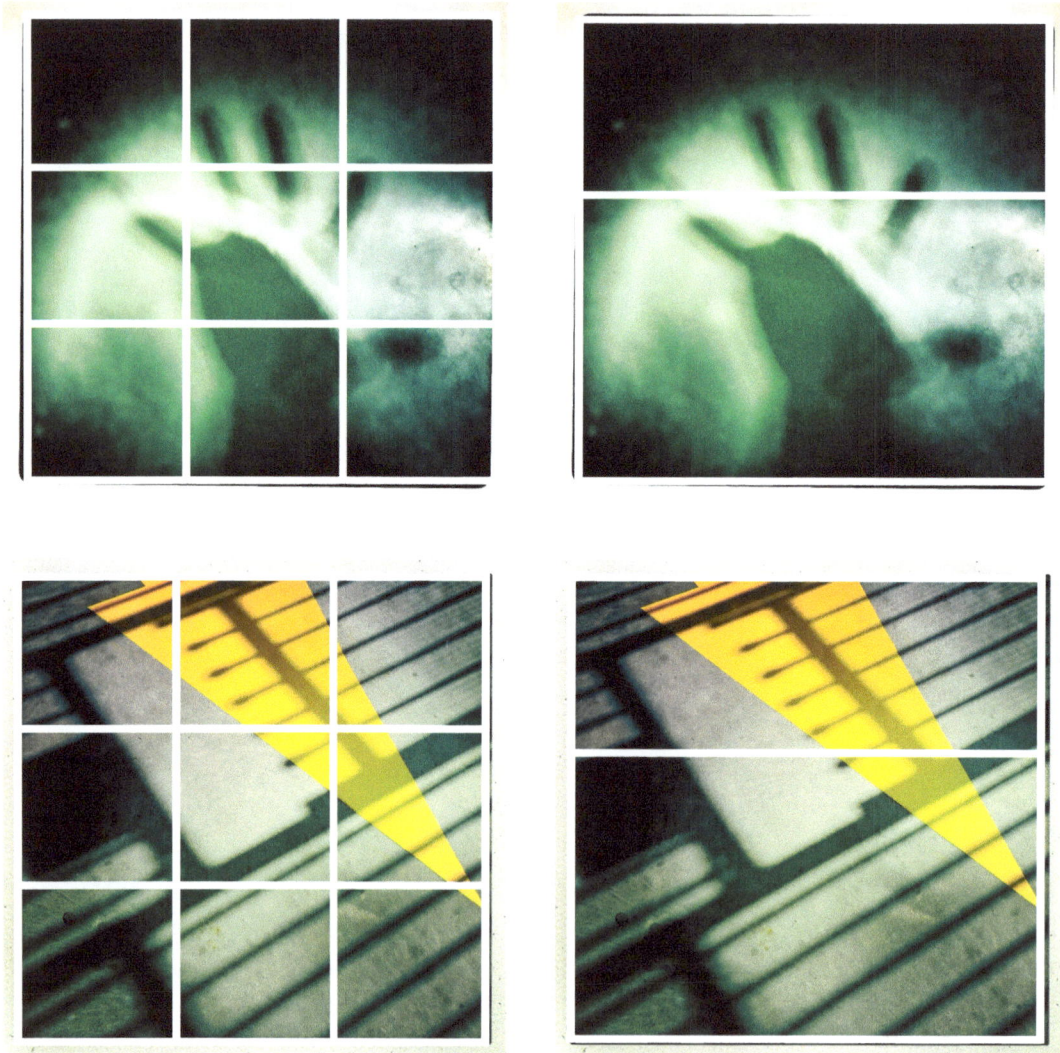

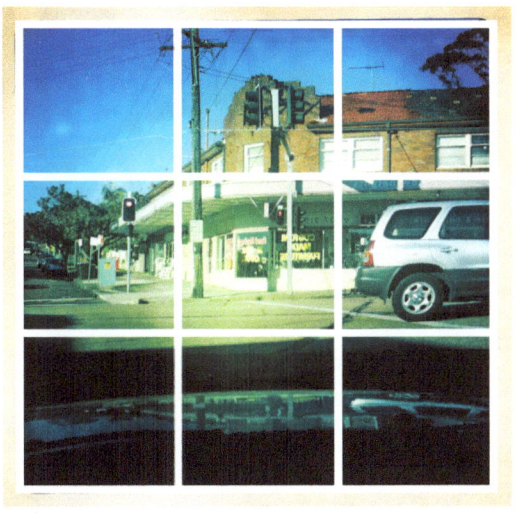
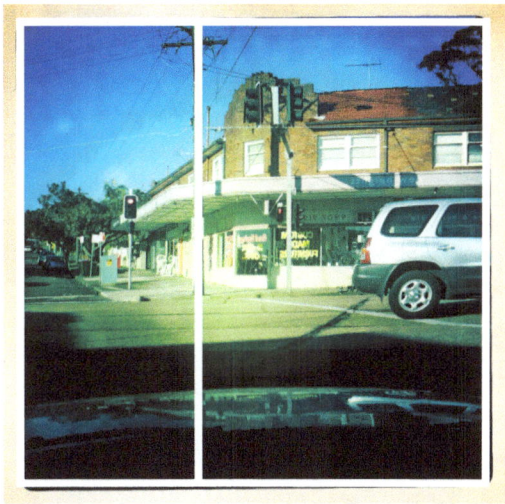
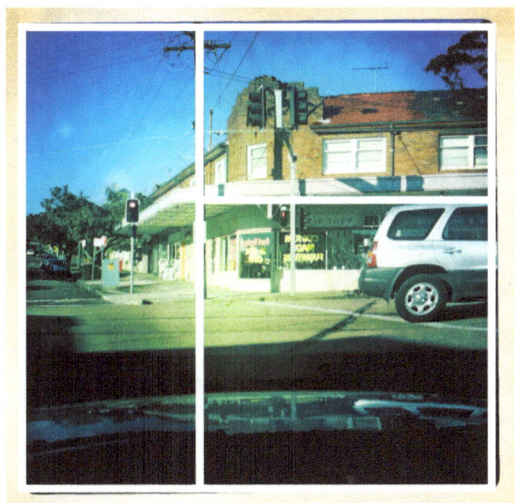
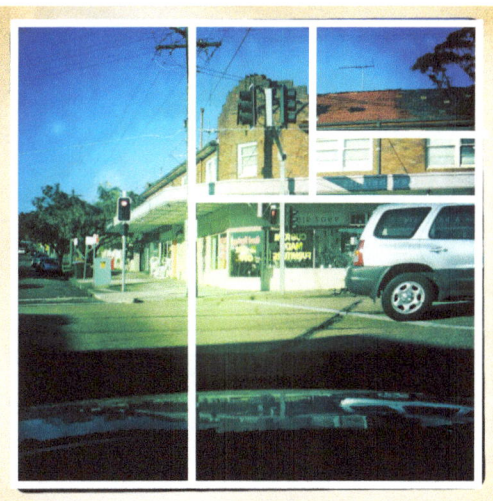

Composition within a square is different to *composition* within a rectangle or a panorama. I have noticed square images are more tolerant of *central composition* than the other image formats.

This is good news for uneducated photographers as this is the default *compositional* tendency of nearly everyone, at least in the beginning of their photographic education.

Composing absolutely centre is nearly always *boring* and kills the *flow of the image*.

One of the tricks is to give the viewer the opportunity to visually wander through the photograph. This is called *flow*. Sometimes we create photographs with no flow at all: they have *closed composition,* not *open composition.*

Chinese panoramic landscape painting placed great emphasis on offering the viewer a journey through their inspired landscapes. The viewer might walk by a lake, stop at a tavern, and catch a ferry across a river, meeting people and noticing beautiful trees and rocks and birds on the way, before coming to rest in the distant village.

This thinking is a little lost in western art, but is well worth following, and if you choose, so is doing the opposite.

On the next spread, I have contrasted two photographs: one stops *flow* dead, it nearly leaps off the page and attacks you. There is nowhere to go. The other is *flow*-full. Though both use a similar *colour palette*, their effect is so different.

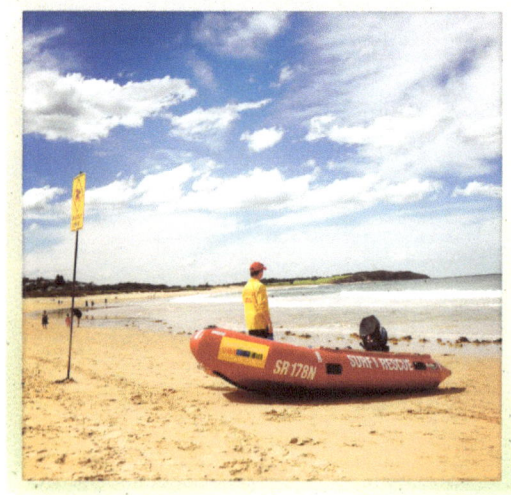

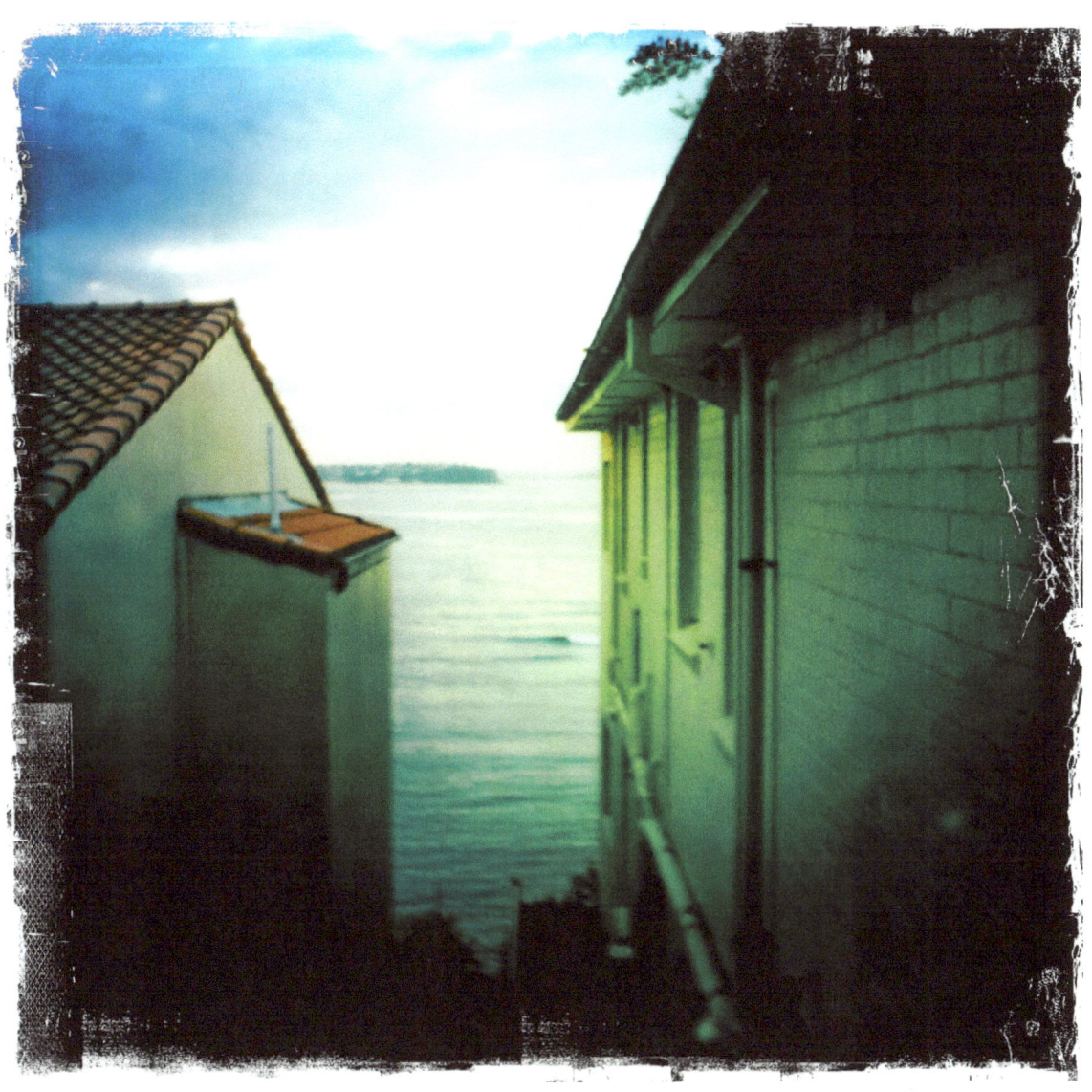

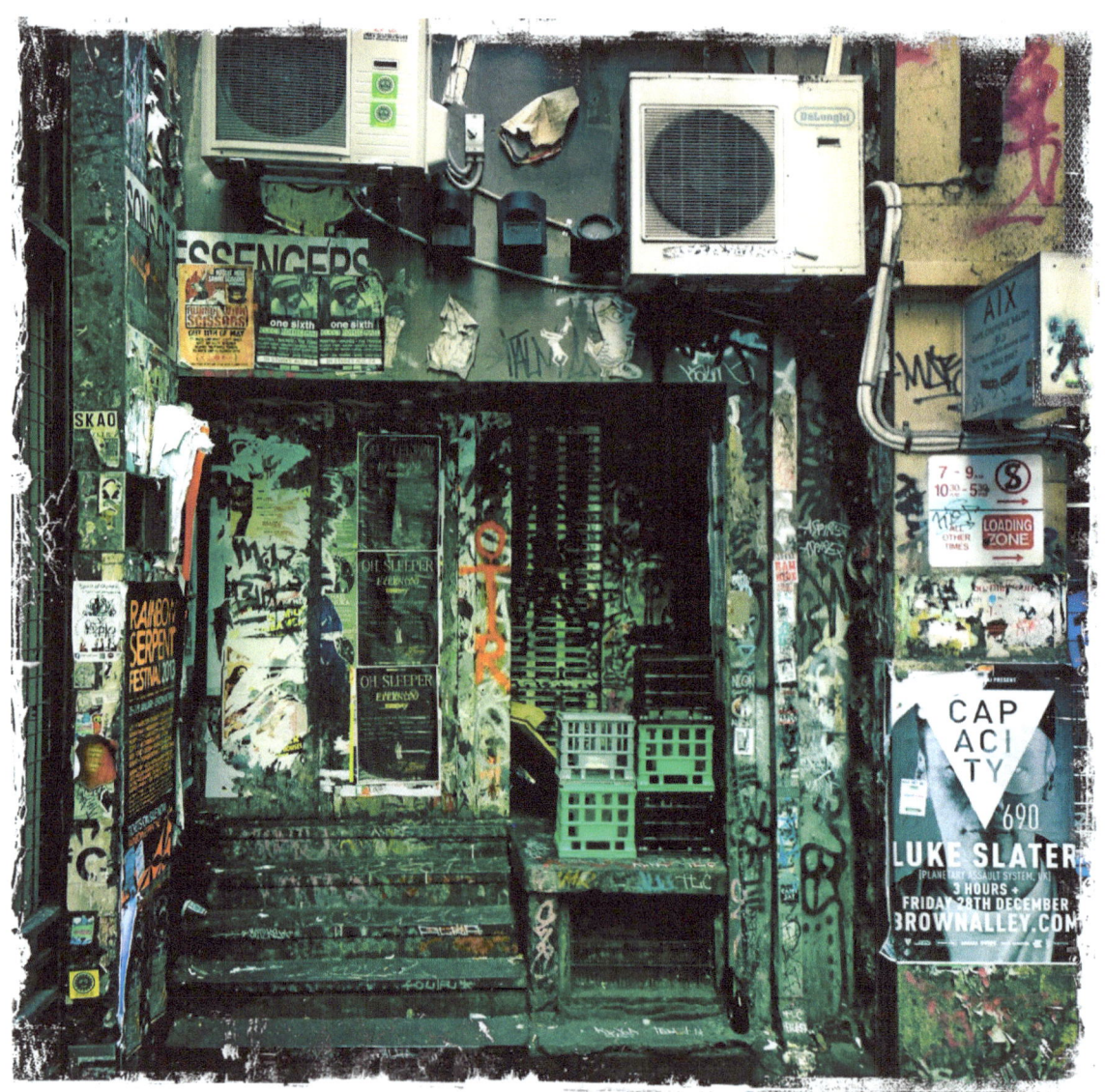

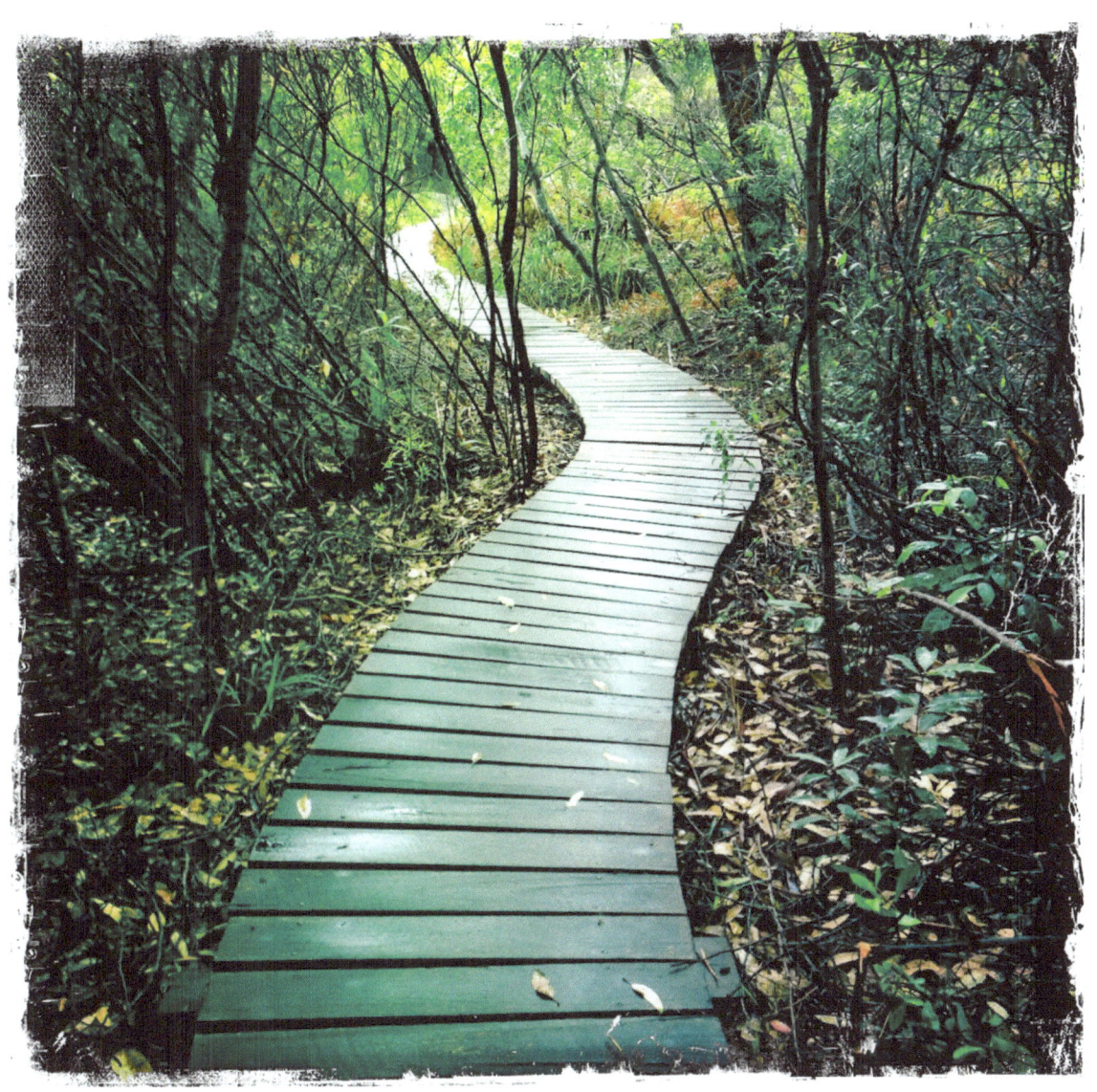

Nostalgia is one of those palliative human emotional conditions that has no future, only a past. Retro is its accomplice. Photographs have a lot to answer for when it comes to outbreaks of nostalgia.

This photograph, with the help of a filter called "Memory", reminds me of the photographs that filled shoe-boxes and sometimes found their way into albums when I was a child. This was a much simpler time when the world was a nicer and simpler place and smartphones were not yet invented.

Father and daughter and grandmother are out on a boat. Major the dog is swimming after them, such a faithful dog is he.

The girl is my sister actually and I took the photograph on the Kodak camera that I was given when I was eight. I found the photo when going through some old stuff in the attic. This was one of our summer holidays by the ocean. Dad built the clinker boat himself and it had a smelly outboard motor. He took turns in giving each of the family a spin on the boat. It was such fun and we all admired Major.

The seaweed smelled and was full of flies. Dad used to have fun with us about crocodiles in the lake and drop bears in the trees. We had a lot of fun scaring my cousin from overseas about the drop bears that jumped out of the trees at night and bit you on the neck. Drop bears do not exist, really.

Gran and Mum used to make picnic lunches and on a good day we got sweets too.

Nostalgia: rose coloured smoke-screen or a reflection on what was good. It can be either or both, often not announcing that you are altering your memory. To check if you are overdoing or not getting enough nostalgia, look up the *Southampton Nostalgia Scale*.

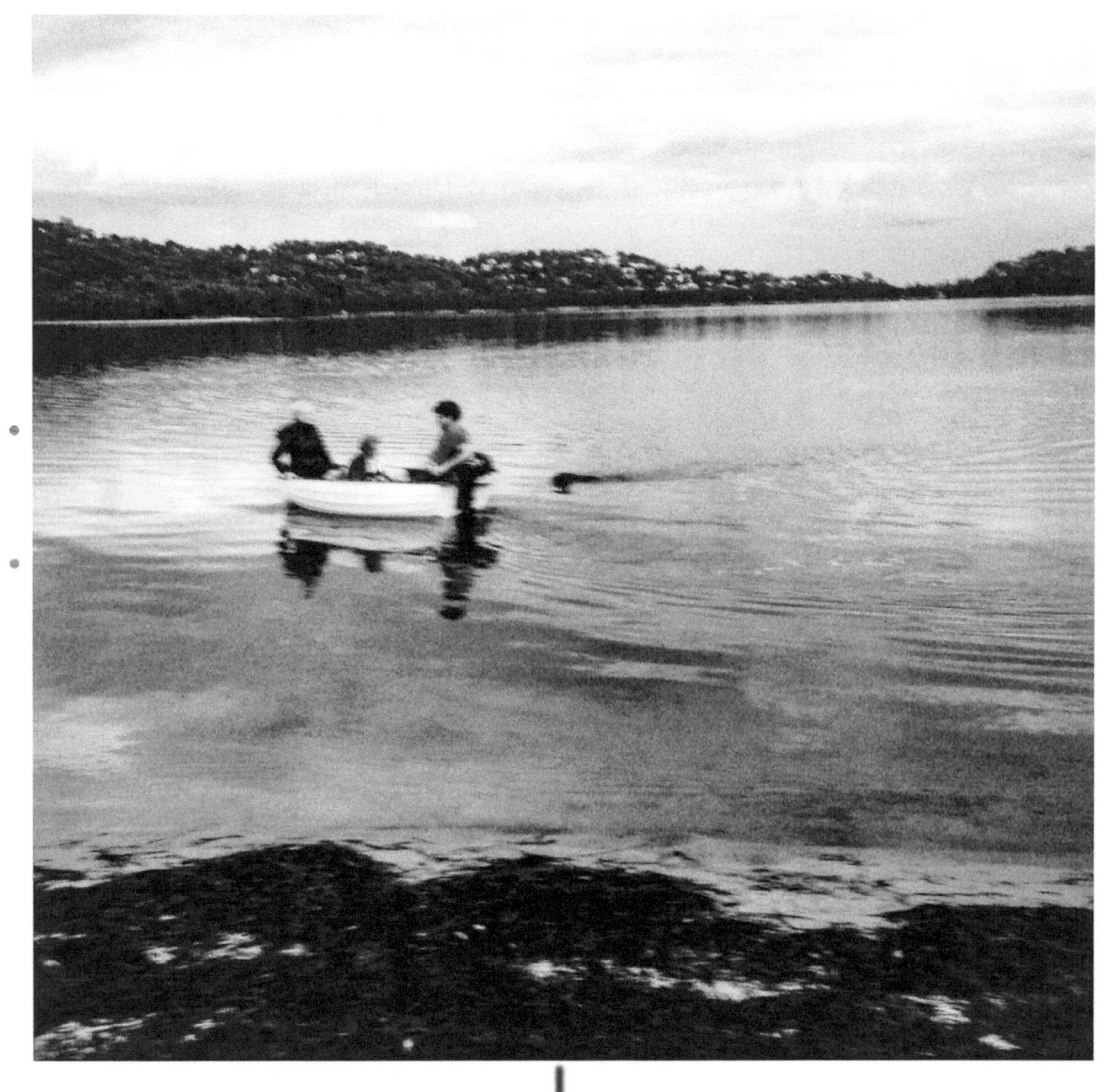

I photographed a wedding with my proper camera and all the pro-photography trappings.

My thousand dollar *speedlight* overheated and shut down just as the rings were being exchanged. Luckily, I had enabled the overheating shutdown feature otherwise it would now be e-waste.

My second *speedlight* (*flash* if you prefer), well used, died. My *wireless flash trigger* also died so I used the last still working *flash* attached to the camera with a coiled *flash* connector cable that dated from the time before *wireless flash triggers* were made in China.

I held the *flash* unit in one hand and the camera in the other with a coiled cable connecting them.

I did this to get the *flash off the camera. Flash On Camera* ALWAYS gives bad results, unless you are using a *Ring Flash* properly. *Flash Off Camera* gives you a chance.

I got through the day as I understand photography enough to improvise on the go and importantly, not appear to the client to be losing it.

I got through also as I brought a spare camera with spare lenses and spare batteries and spare flashes, and a coiled *flash* cable, and a small screwdriver for changing the batteries on my *wireless flash trigger*. But, alas, no *spare wireless flash trigger* (still annoyed!).

Hairdressers have *bad hair days,* I was having a bad photography day.

I gave enough good photographs to the couple (meaning the bride) so that I did not have to jump on a plane and leave the country.

Towards the end of the day, I was so annoyed with my "real" camera gear, I joined in with the crowd who had their smartphones out en masse.

Guess which of my cameras created my most popular photograph that day?

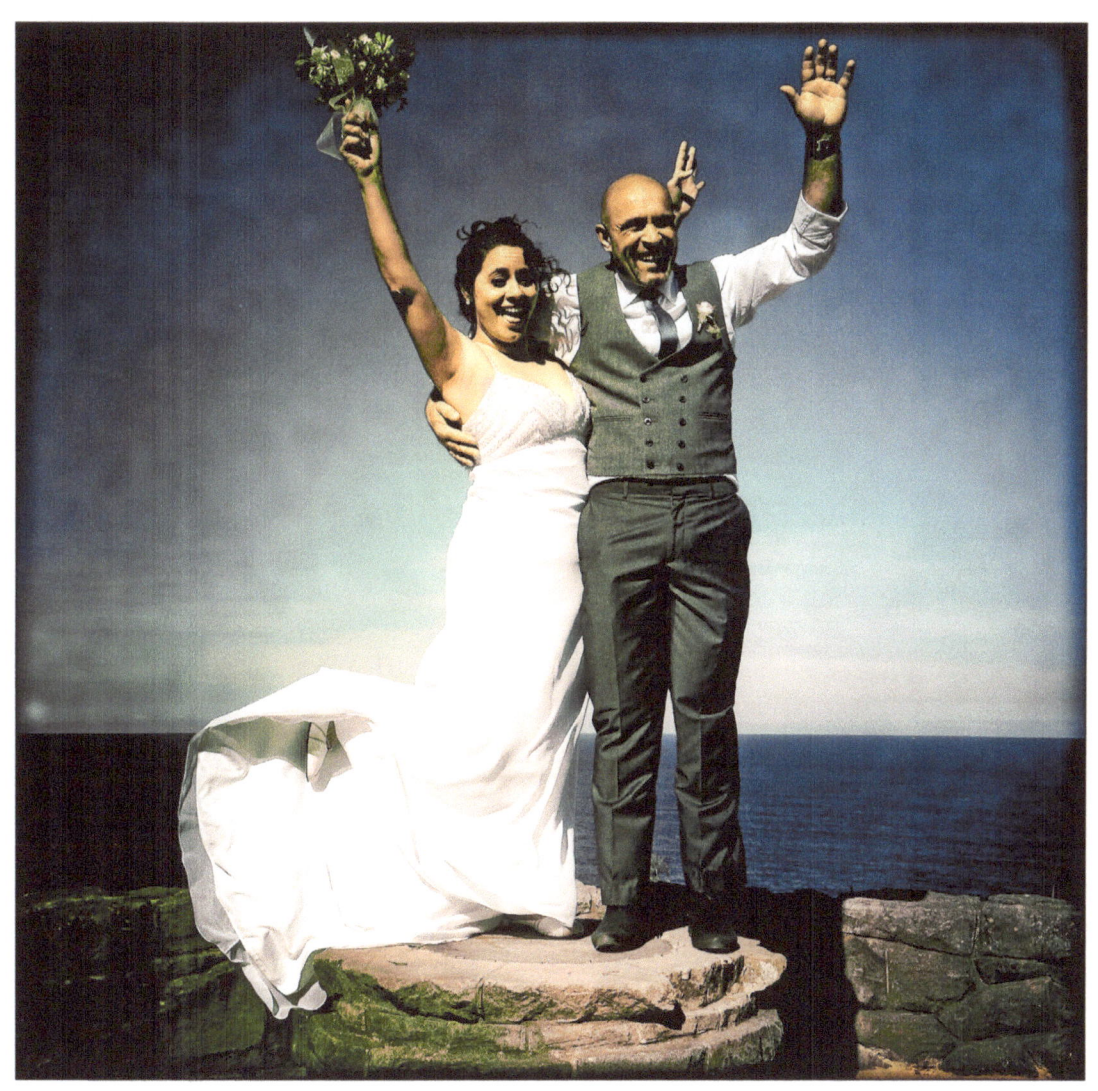

It is usual in *Hipstamatic* circles to specify the lens and film filters used. For example a *Hipstamatic* photo might be accompanied with: Johnny S Lens, Kodot Grizzled Film, Triple Crown Flash.

Should you use the *Hipstamatic* app you will discover what filters I used, and at times got stuck on. You will also find your own favourites on which you may also get stuck on for a while.

Much the same technique thing used to happen in film days with descriptions such as: *Kodachrome 64 Daylight* film, 1/125, f11, exposed at ASA80, 81A warming filter.

The images in this book are largely as shot, though some are edited in the app, some in other apps and some in *Photoshop*. All images in the paper book have been adjusted so they print well.

If you want to delve further into technical aspects of photography, "proper" or smartphone photography, please visit my website.

Details of technique are important and if you are serious you will come to terms with technique. However, on their own, the minutiae of technique can become a labyrinthine journey in which you will miss the point of photography entirely.

The point of photography is to create photographs that move and excite yourself and move and excite others. You may even wish that your photographs could bring about positive change.

The grail then, is discovering for yourself what makes a photograph work visually as a design and most importantly, as words and sentences of emotional communication. It is learning how to create photographs that deliver a visceral emotional response.

I have been on this grail quest for some time. I hope you are also a fellow traveller on this quest.

This book is a witnessing of how a mobile telephone with a camera has revolutionised my photography. Look around and you will see it has revolutionised everyone else's also.

Where photography is going is exciting. Stay tuned!

I suggest you visit *Hipstamatic*. There is more to Hipstamatic than just the camera app.

http://hipstamatic.com

I also want to share an outstanding source of *Hipstamatic* information, inspiration and community:

http://hipstography.com/en/

The site creator, rather like myself, is fascinated with what *Hipstamatic* does for photography and likewise, has a desire to share this fascination and passion.

Finally, please visit my own website for:

- Photography courses, books and epubs
- Advance information on new publications
- Writings on Photography
- Eye-candy

http://www.luminere.com

Good Bye for now, and Good Luck

Orlando Luminere
2016

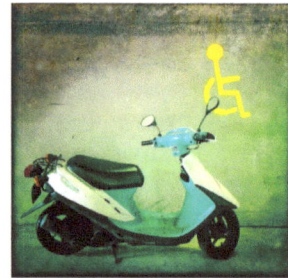

I found the scooter photo in the depths of my social media web page, alas, at low resolution. This is as large as I can print it, the DAM equivalent of crashing my motorcycle.

www.ingramcontent.com/pod-product-compliance
Lightning Source LLC
Chambersburg PA
CBHW050720180526
45159CB00003B/1087